Restored

A HANDBOOK FOR FEMALE SURVIVORS OF DOMESTIC ABUSE WITH A CHRISTIAN PERSPECTIVE

Editor **Esther Sweetman**

First Edition - First published in Great Britain in 2019

Published by Restored

ISBN: 978-1-9164908-0-2
British National Bibliography - application pending.

Editor: Esther Sweetman, BA (Hons), Dip CS, MA, MSc
Sub-editor: Mandy Marshall, BA (Hons)
Copy editor: Deborah Hewitt, BA (Hons), Dip SW
Cover and layout design by David Potter (david-potter.co.uk)
Printed by printed.com who are certified by the Forest Stewardship Council.

Restored is an international Christian alliance working to transform relationships and end violence against women. We raise awareness and train churches to identify and respond appropriately to domestic abuse in their congregations. We engage men in the response to violence against women in our First Man Standing Campaign. We provide resources to support both churches and survivors.

Restored is a registered charity in England and Wales, Charity No: 1136774.
Restored is a private limited company, registered in England and Wales at Companies House, London. Company No: 7243226.

To order copies:

Restored
PO Box 447
Teddington, Middlesex
TW11 1AY

Tel: +44 (0)20 3906 3922
Email: info@restoredrelationships.org
www.restoredrelationships.org

Twitter.com/Rest0red
Facebook.com/RestoredRelationships
www.Instagram.com/restoredrelationships/

To donate to Restored: give.net/Restored

Dedication

This handbook is dedicated to all survivors of domestic abuse who are courageously rebuilding their lives day by day and step by step. Your determination to seek a better life for yourselves and your children and your bravery and resilience in the face of barriers and challenges are respected and honoured.

Acknowledgments

We are grateful to Cross Pollinate who originally funded the start of the Survivors' Network from which this handbook has grown.

A sincere thank you to Bain & Co, a global management consulting firm, who provided pivotal funding that allowed Restored to begin this essential project.

Restored is extremely grateful to each of the contributors to this handbook. Their individual experience and knowledge has brought a wealth of information and support to survivors. The willingness of each author to share their expertise has created a handbook which is a unique and invaluable resource for those affected by domestic abuse.

We would like to extend a huge thank you to Deborah Hewitt for her time and commitment in sharing her expert copy editing skills and providing helpful and knowledgeable suggestions. Many thanks also goes to Lucy McDonald for giving her time to proofread and provide useful feedback.

Thank you to Dave Potter for the excellent design of the handbook and his dedication to this project. He brought the chapters to life, enabling the information and key points to be easily read.

Finally, thank you to Esther Sweetman whose passion, commitment and concern to see survivors of domestic abuse recover, heal, and move forward with their lives, has brought this handbook to fruition. Restored is indebted to Esther for the production and delivery of this handbook. Thank you.

Mandy Marshall
Co-Founder and Co-Director, Restored

Contents

FOREWORD

Mandy Marshall Co-Founder and Co-Director of Restored

It was a beautiful and hot day in Zimbabwe. The sun was blinding. I'd just finished speaking at a church in a rural area when a woman came up to me and, through the translator, asked to speak to me. In the darkness of her mud hut home we sat down and she disclosed the horrific abuse that her Christian husband was perpetrating on her. I asked her if she had informed the Pastor of the church. 'Yes', she replied, 'he told me I should submit more, pray more and stop nagging him.' I felt the anger rise in me. She continued, 'I've done all of that and nothing has changed. You're the expert – what more can I do?'. My heart felt like it had shattered into a million pieces and it took all that I could to muster not to cry. This wasn't her fault. It wasn't her problem and yet the Pastor, who was ill-equipped to respond, had placed the responsibility on her. I advised her as best I could on how to keep herself safe, reassured her that this was not her fault, that her husband was to blame and that he was the one that needed to change.

I left feeling furious that what should be a place of sanctuary (the church) had added to the problem. It had to stop. I raged at God, 'Why are you allowing this to happen?' and 'Why aren't you doing anything about it?' My questions rebounded back at me, 'Why wasn't I doing anything about it?' I argued with God, 'Who am I to try and change the global church and

address this issue?' The answer came back, 'Who are you not to try?'.

It was this experience that motivated me to co-found Restored with Peter Grant in 2010. At Restored we aim to answer two questions: 'Where is the Church?' and 'Where are the men?' when it comes to ending domestic abuse. Restored exists to raise awareness that domestic abuse happens in churches too and to resource and equip the church to respond appropriately and effectively to domestic abuse. Restored does this by providing information packs to churches on how to address domestic abuse appropriately; we train church members, we work with men through the First Man Standing programme and we provide a safe online network for Christian survivors of abuse.

It is the work with Christian survivors of abuse that has prompted this handbook. As Restored became known in the Christian sector, we started to receive emails and phone calls from Christian survivors of domestic abuse sharing their story with us, wanting to know where to get help and support, and also thanking us for simply existing and addressing the issue of domestic abuse within the church.

Esther Sweetman came along as an expert volunteer at Restored three years ago and developed the Survivors' Network into what it is today. Esther, a qualified counsellor and social researcher with training in theology, brought her professional experience and expertise to the role. Over the last few years Esther has written many blogs for survivors addressing emotional recovery, theological questions and practical challenges. She has encouraged survivors to share their stories in their own words, which have been published on Restored's website www.restoredrelationships.org. There was such a volume of material being produced that we thought it was an amazing opportunity to adapt it into a handbook for survivors. This was the start of the process that led to recruiting experts in their field to contribute topical chapters for a handbook for Christian survivors of domestic abuse that would deal with a wide range of issues in one book.

I am very grateful to all the authors who have contributed to this handbook. Thank you for your time, energy and effort you have put into sharing your wisdom, experience and skills in writing in an easily accessible format. It is very much appreciated. Thank you.

This handbook is important as it is unique in its focus on Christian female survivors of domestic abuse in the UK. As far as we are aware, it's the first of its kind (although do get in touch if you know of others, as we'd love to hear from you!). We hope that this handbook will provide practical help, useful tips and also encouragement as you process what you have been through and step out of the darkness that has been binding you and into the light of new hope and life. Jesus came to give you life in all its fullness.

Recovering from abuse is not an easy journey. It can be a long struggle, but we hope that this book will help you as you move on and forward in your new life. It will also be a useful tool for friends, family and church leaders, as it gives an insight into the realities of domestic abuse.

I hope this handbook will provide you with hope and life. I'm so grateful to Esther and all the contributors to the handbook for making this a reality. May many lives be restored through your efforts.
Thank you.

Mandy Marshall
Co-Founder and Co-Director, Restored

INTRODUCTION

Esther Sweetman
Survivors' Network Coordinator, Restored

All survivors of domestic abuse know that the challenges when leaving an abuser are many and varied, and that healing and recovery are not immediate. The road to recovery is not easy or straightforward; there are many bumps and a few minefields to navigate. The purpose of this handbook is to make this road a little easier for you and to also give you hope and encouragement along the way. You are not alone and your experiences are shared by many who have travelled this road before you and are now living contented and satisfying lives.

This handbook is meant to be a resource for Christian female survivors of domestic abuse in the UK. However, many of the topics discussed and information provided will be beneficial no matter where you live (even if the local services may be different) and whether you practise a particular faith or not.

The chapters are separated into themes that map the road to recovery. However, as we are all on a different stretch of this road, you can dip in and out at the appropriate point for you. This handbook is therefore meant to be a reference book, to read as and when you need it. This is the 1st Edition, with the aim that it will be revised and updated regularly.

Currently, this handbook is unique amongst domestic abuse survivor resources, not only for the breadth of topics covered, but also because it deals specifically with issues facing those of the Christian faith. Each topic also provides links to further resources and support. Every chapter is written by an expert in their field with many years of experience. To get to know the authors better, please refer to the *Introducing the Authors* section in the Appendix.

The first section or theme of the handbook is called **Managing the Practical Realities after Leaving a Male Abuser**. Before survivors have the opportunity to deal with our own personal healing and recovery immediately after leaving an abuser, we will have many practical challenges to deal with: finding new accommodation, putting safety and security measures in place, dealing with all aspects of a divorce (finances and children), budgeting/finances and potentially returning to work. These concerns are diverse, so we have helpfully addressed them together in one book so that you don't have to look in a variety of different places to get support on these various issues.

Once the practical issues are dealt with, we can move on to our own **Healing and Recovery after Leaving a Male Abuser** and this is the second theme of this handbook. Supporting our children, managing our own physical and emotional health and starting to focus on our own self care are incredibly important at this stage. We also wanted to take up the challenge of addressing topics that are purposefully overlooked, minimised or dismissed by many due to their difficult subject matter. Therefore we have chapters that deal with sexual exploitation in relationships as well as the link between pornography use/infidelity and domestic abuse.

This handbook also provides a chapter on concrete and practical healing practices for your individual personality and interest areas and a chapter that looks to building your new life, giving you hope and excitement for what is to come.

Finally, the last section addresses **Theological Issues Relating to Domestic Abuse**. Questions regarding what the bible has to say about domestic abuse, divorce, justice and forgiveness may have come up for you at any stage on your road to recovery and we want to provide you with an opportunity to engage with these issues. There is no guilt or shame in leaving an abuser. We want you to feel confident in your decision to leave and to feel loved, valued and cared for by God.

We hope that this handbook will serve you well now and into the future.

Esther Sweetman
Survivors' Network Coordinator

Currently, this handbook is unique amongst domestic abuse survivor resources

PART 1 OUTLINE OF DOMESTIC ABUSE

CHAPTER 1
What is Domestic Abuse?

What constitutes abuse? This simple question represents one of the greatest challenges to understanding domestic abuse. The most common understanding of relationship abuse in the United Kingdom is depicted in the news as stories and images of physical violence. This often leads us to believe that only physical abuse is a valid form of domestic violence. This gross misconception dramatically impacts not only the statistics on this vital topic, but most importantly the lived reality of abused women and their opportunities for recovery.

The UK Government defines domestic abuse as *"Any incident or pattern of incidents of controlling, coercive or threatening behaviour, violence or abuse between those aged 16 or over who are or have been intimate partners or family members regardless of gender or sexuality. This can encompass but is not limited to the* *following types of abuse: psychological, physical, sexual, financial and emotional"*[1].

A pattern of power and control over another is the central concept of domestic abuse. *"Controlling behaviour is: a range of acts designed to make a person subordinate and/or dependent by isolating* them from sources of support, exploiting their resources and capacities for personal gain, depriving them of the means needed for independence, resistance and escape and regulating their everyday behaviour. Coercive behaviour is: an act or a pattern of acts of assault, threats, humiliation and intimidation or other abuse that is used to harm, punish, or frighten their victim"[2].

To gain a deeper understanding of what actually constitutes abuse we will now explore the various types of domestic abuse mentioned above, and will also include a review of spiritual abuse which is often overlooked.

It is important to know that all types of abuse are often unpredictable, with periods of calm where the abuser reaffirms his love and promises to change, and then cycles back to anger and control over his partner. (Please refer to chapter 2: The Cycle of Abuse for a fuller explanation).

Emotional Abuse

Emotional abuse falls under the wider category of psychological abuse and is a form of intimate partner violence that is often described by survivors as more destructive than being physically hit and can have devastating long-term effects. It can be defined as: "repetitive attitudes and behaviours that result in tearing someone down or inhibiting her growth... and is usually accompanied by a lack of awareness, a lack of responsibility, and a lack of change" on behalf of the abusive partner[3]. Emotional abuse is

a devastating act of domestic violence which leaves a woman deeply shamed in her identity—her sense of being or self—as her partner's "emotional abuse systematically degrades, diminishes, and [may] eventually destroy the personhood of the abused"[4]. Over time a woman may internalise her partner's abuse, believing what he says, and believing that her perception of reality and her feelings are wrong. This is called crazy-making—or emotional gaslighting— as the abusive partner denies his abusive behaviour towards his partner, while presenting himself in public as charismatic and 'normal'.

> Emotional abuse often precedes physical abuse in relationships and should be considered a serious act of violence.

Emotional abuse can also include verbal abuse and can be overt such as: yelling, angry outbursts, making threats, blaming, belittling, isolation, controlling what you wear, constant judging and criticising, name-calling, and ordering; or covert abuse such as: lying, denying, minimising, forgetting, blocking and diverting, discounting, neglect, abandonment, withholding or making jokes. Finally, one of the most essential points to be aware of is that emotional abuse often precedes physical abuse in relationships and should be considered a serious act of violence from one partner to another.

Physical Abuse

While emotional abuse is often a precursor to physical violence, it is usually when a woman's body bears the bruises inflicted by her partner that most people would acknowledge domestic violence

has occurred. Indeed, it is perhaps the easiest type of abuse to recognise and document when bruises and broken bones can be reported to a doctor, for instance. In the UK two women a week are murdered by their partner or former partner on average, or one women every three days[5]. While many women are worried about heart disease or cancer, a significant threat to a woman's health remains firmly in the form of physical violence at the hands of her male partner.

There are many types of physical abuse, including—but not limited to—intentional acts of hair pulling, slapping, hitting, punching, slamming a woman against something, throwing her across the room, choking or strangling her, burning her, or having a knife or gun used against her. Additionally, an abuser will often make threats of violence to cause fear and assert control over his female partner, as in emotional abuse. While the frequency and severity of physical violence can vary in any abusive relationship over time, it is essential to take any and every threat seriously. Alongside this devastating reality of women's lives, it is critical to know that a woman is *most likely* to be murdered by a partner *after* she leaves the abuser. It should not be a surprise, then, that many women remain with an abuser to protect themselves and any children they may have.

Sexual Abuse

Sexual abuse is undeniably a prolific form of relationship abuse. According to the UK's Office for National Statistics (2017) for 45% of rape victims in the UK the offender was a partner or ex-partner.[6] Sexual violence and abuse is defined as "any behaviour of a sexual nature which is unwanted and takes place without consent or understanding". Sexual abuse includes, but is certainly not limited to, marital rape, attacks on sexual parts of the body, forcing sex after physical violence has occurred, or treating one in a sexually demeaning manner. (Please refer to chapter 18: *Dealing with Sexual Exploitation in Relationships* for further discussion on this topic.)

Again, as we think about abuse and its essential use of power and control over another person, it is important to remember that there are various forms of force. An abuser may employ physical force, but psychological or emotional coercion, manipulation and threats of harm, and other forms of intimidation, are additional types of force utilised to make a victim comply. Here it is critical to recognise that compliance is not the same as consent; and explicit consent must be given: unwanted sexual contact, behaviour or acts constitute sexual violence. In addition to physical sexual acts, sexual abuse also includes an individual's right to control the context and circumstances in which sexual activity occurs, and their access to birth control and condoms.

As with emotional abuse, a significant step in addressing sexual abuse is the recognition that all experiences of this type of intimate partner violence be considered acts of abuse. Sexual abuse is a particularly violating encounter in the embodied, private nature of this act. Additionally, female survivors of sexual abuse are often blamed by the public—rather than blaming the perpetrator—as though her choice of clothing, drink, or agreeing to go on a date justifies her being sexually abused.

It is critical to understand that, unless an individual gives explicit and unforced verbal consent to sexual activity, all such sexual acts must be considered sexual abuse. This illustrates a frequent issue within domestic abuse: the notion that female victims are somehow to blame for the abusive actions of their male partners. Such a damaging belief is embedded in our culture—and often in our faith communities—and represents an imperative call for truth to be declared: all forms of domestic violence are *always* the responsibility of the abuser.

Financial Abuse

One of the invisible weapons in intimate partner violence is that of finances and it is one of the least recognised types of relational violence. According to UK's Women's Aid, financial abuse happens at some point for the vast majority of survivors.[7] Here we start to see that the coercive and controlling behaviour of abusers is not simple, but incredibly complex and interrelated; in fact, most survivors experience more than one form of abuse from their abuser. Manipulation and control over a partner's finances are frequently used to prevent a woman from acquiring, spending, or keeping money or other forms of financial resources. As an unseen mode of isolation, financial abuse effectively cuts her off from accessing means to leave the abuser and to recover. Indeed, one of the primary reasons a woman does not leave her male abuser is financial abuse, trapping her in a position of dependence on her male partner.

This extremely common tactic includes both subtle and more overt instances of abusive behaviours that represent serious betrayals of a person's rights. Some examples of the insidious actions of financial abuse women experience are: having credit cards and loans taken out in her name without her consent; using her bank cards without her knowledge; being given an allowance and having purchases closely watched; manipulating her to sign loans, mortgages, or other financial documents; threatening her to coerce her into financial decisions, and preventing her from working or demanding she quit. These illustrations of financial abuse depict the many methods by which many abusers seek to control and coerce women into dependency and take away their self-sufficiency. Such abuse, though in some ways documentable, remains largely outside the public sphere of legal justice and so is a powerful tool that can devastate women through a lack of food, medical care, clothing, and sustainable housing, resulting in poverty and homelessness. These barriers to meeting a woman's fundamental human needs severely impair a survivor's access to security and safety either within an abusive relationship or afterwards if she is able to leave.

Spiritual Abuse

Many women of faith who experience relational abuse will encounter the deep wounds of spiritual abuse. The significant factor to keep in mind—as in all forms of abuse—is that abuse is about using *power and control* over another person, and anyone can behave abusively. With this in mind, spiritual abuse in relationships can be seen as the use of power and authority to dominate or control a partner through the use of spiritual, biblical or other religious practices that minimise, deny, or harm a partner's right to full equality[8].

Spiritual abuse consists of the abuser using theology or scripture to: deny a female partner the right to make decisions within the relationship or family; bar her from pursuing leadership in the church or public spheres; denounce her personhood as less than his; blame her for not submitting to his authority; threaten to abandon her for spiritual reasons; declare her thoughts, beliefs or actions sinful or ungodly; or refuse to let her separate or divorce due to his abuse. (Please refer to chapter 26: *Spiritual Abuse* for further discussion on this topic.)

While such examples are not exhaustive, spiritual abuse is essentially the act of justifying one's abusive behaviours through spiritual or biblical means, the effect of which is the breakdown of the survivor's identity as the beloved of God by attacking her perceptions of God and herself as God's good daughter.

> Abuse is about using power and control over another person, and anyone can behave abusively.

> **TOP TIP**
> Remember, the abuse you suffered was not your fault. You are loved and valued by God.

References

1 Home Office (2013). *Information for Local Areas on the change to the Definition of Domestic Violence and Abuse*
https://assets.publishing.service.gov.uk/government/uploads/system/uploads/attachment_data/file/142701/guide-on-definition-of-dv.pdf (accessed online 26/10/2018).

2 Ibid.

3 Vernick,Leslie. (2013). *The Emotionally Destructive Marriage: How to Find Your Voice and Reclaim Your Hope.* Colorado Springs: WaterBrook Press.

4 Evans, Patricia. (1996). *The Verbally Abusive Relationship: How to Recognize it and How to Respond,* **expanded 2nd ed**. Holbrook: Adams Media Corporation.

5 Coleman and Osborne, (2010); Povey,(ed.)(2004, 2005); Home Office, (1999); Department of Health, (2005); Office for National Statistics (2015).

6 Office for National Statistics. (2017). *Sexual offences in England and Wales: year ending March 2017*.
https://www.ons.gov.uk/peoplepopulationandcommunity/crimeandjustice/articles/sexualoffencesinenglandandwales/yearendingmarch2017#how-are-victims-and-perpetrators-related (accessed online 26/10/2018).

7 Women's Aid (2017) *What is Financial Abuse?* https://www.womensaid.org.uk/information-support/what-is-domestic-abuse/financial-abuse/ (accessed online 26/10/2018).

8 Miles, Al. (2002). *Violence in Families: What Every Christian Needs to Know.* Minneapolis: Augsburg Press.

Notes

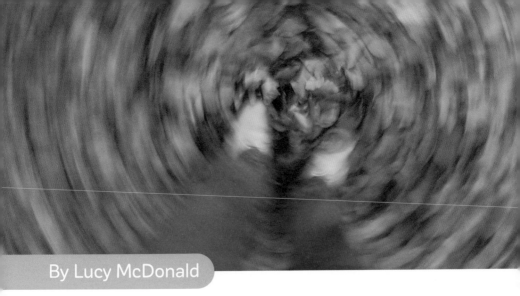

By Lucy McDonald

CHAPTER 2

The Cycle of Abuse

This chapter looks at a theory that has been researched and written about, in the world of domestic violence, for nearly forty years. It is called 'The Cycle of Abuse'. Whether you are still with your abusive partner or have left, ideas such as these can be helpful in recognising that you are not alone in your experiences. Many other women have suffered through the same cycle, at the hands of a different man. This knowledge can be a helpful reminder that the perpetrator is the cause of domestic abuse, not you.

This chapter outlines and explains the three main parts of the cycle and looks at how you can move forward.

Cycle (sī-kəl) *noun*
A course or series of events or operations that recur regularly and usually lead back to the starting point. (Definition from Merriam-Webster, online)

In 1979 Lenore E. Walker, a psychologist, came up with the term 'The Cycle of Abuse'. This theory outlines how stages of an abusive relationship often follow a similar pattern and keep repeating themselves in the same order. What's important to know is that, in her research, Walker makes it clear that there 'are no specific personality traits which would suggest a victim-prone personality for the women' (Walker, 1983).

All relationships are unique so the Cycle of Abuse can look different from one abuser to the next. It's also important to be aware that these stages don't follow a particular timeframe; they can happen over days, weeks or months and the phases can also last for any length of time.

There are three main stages which make up the Cycle and they usually progress in the order outlined below; however, a relationship will usually begin with the honeymoon stage. If it didn't, and had skipped straight to him being abusive, you probably wouldn't have entered into the relationship in the first place.

The honeymoon period is wonderful but it is unrealistic to expect it to carry on for the entirety of a relationship because a relationship is two imperfect human beings muddling through life together. This means it is impossible to always be on your best behaviour. However, what happens after the honeymoon period is what sets apart an abusive from a healthy relationship.

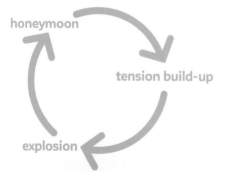

The three stages are referred to as: tension building, explosion and honeymoon.

Tension building:

When the honeymoon period is over in an abusive relationship, tension can begin to creep in. Issues start to arise, for example arguments about finances, housework and employment, and communication starts to breaks down. In a healthy relationship these can be dealt with equally, with neither partner asserting control. However, what's happening in an abusive relationship is that his behaviour escalates because he feels like he is losing control and he starts to engage in abusive behaviours to reassert his control over you.

What he might do:
- Shout, scream, or give you the silent treatment.
- Goad you – try to get you to argue back.
- Call you names or destroy your belongings.
- Threaten you e.g. to report you to social services if you have children.
- Accuse you of being unfaithful e.g. having an affair.

What you might do:
- Calm him down by attempting to minimise his abusive behaviour.
- Make excuses for his behaviour i.e. 'he is tired and stressed, if I hadn't done X he wouldn't have done Y.'
- Try to keep the peace by becoming totally compliant to his wants and wishes.
- Try to nurture him.
- Withdraw from the situation.

It is important to understand that he will see anything you are doing as an attack on his power and control, even though that's probably the last thing you are trying to do. As this is his perception, his behaviour will continue to be focused on maintaining or re-gaining power and control, and further abusive behaviours will be directed at you.

Sometimes survivors refer to this stage as 'walking on eggshells' with a continued feeling of dread and a knot in the stomach. It's important to note that there will of course be tension in healthy relationships but what distinguishes them from unhealthy abusive relationships is how the tension is resolved. Could you sit down and talk about how you were feeling with your partner or was he quickly moving to stage two of the cycle?

Acute explosion:

In this second stage there is an explosion which may culminate in physical violence. There might be no way of rationalising his behaviour at this point. The event that led to his explosion might even have been sparked by something external to the relationship. His goal here is for you to feel fully responsible for his abusive behaviour.

What he might do:
- Scream, order, verbally abuse or threaten you.
- Hit, slap, kick, shove, strangle, choke, suffocate or try to drown you.
- Destroy household objects or your belongings.

- Use weapons or objects against you.
- Hurt your children or pets.
- Stop you from leaving e.g. lock you in the house.
- Stalk you if you go out.
- Force you to have sex.

What you might do:
- Try to appease him to keep the peace.
- Feel shame and minimise the abuse.
- Try to hide the truth for the 'sake of the family.'
- Call the police.
- Protect yourself by fighting back.
- Leave the relationship either temporarily or permanently.

At this stage your risk is increasing because his behaviour is getting worse and has the potential to become very violent. Pregnancy or him knowing you are trying to leave will both make your risk even greater.

When this cycle begins to become a part of the abuser's behaviour, the explosions can start off quite small. However, they get worse over time and you may not even realise quite how bad things are becoming. At the beginning you may excuse the small outbursts because you want to keep the peace, but this leads to his explosions worsening because he expects to be excused no matter what his behaviour.

This can be an extremely scary stage of the cycle, though the irony is that, because of the way the cycle rotates, you know that 'good' is coming. Inevitably this

> Sometimes survivors refer to this stage as 'walking on eggshells' with a continued feeling of dread and a knot in the stomach.

19

explosion leads on to the third phase of the cycle which is the honeymoon stage all over again.

Honeymoon Stage:

Generally, we have the honeymoon stage at the beginning of a relationship and *unfortunately* it also comes around time and time again in The Cycle of Abuse. It's the part of the relationship that women stay for because all seems good in the world again; it's a reminder of what has been, how the relationship started and the explosion becomes 'forgotten'. He is sorry, wants the relationship to continue and does not appear to demonstrate abuse at this time. Though it may seem like a 'good' stage of the relationship, it is important to 'remember, in every phase of this abuse cycle, abuse is operating' (Crippen, 2015). The kind of honeymoon behaviour mentioned below is to maintain power and control over you and to keep you in the relationship; it is not a demonstration of real change.

> It is important to 'remember, in every phase of this abuse cycle, abuse is operating'.

What he might do:
- Apologise/make a show of repentance.
- Say he will get support e.g. counselling.
- Buy you gifts/take you on holiday.
- Say it will never happen again.
- Blame it on work/stress/drugs/ alcohol/his childhood.
- Cry.

What you might do:
- Feel relieved.
- Feel happy.
- Forgive him.

- Return to him if you had left the relationship.
- Retract your police statement.
- Take the blame for his behaviour.

In the honeymoon period we again see the perpetrator as the man we fell in love with at the beginning of the relationship. The one who we never imagined would hurt or humiliate us. However, if we look at The Cycle of Abuse as a whole, the person you are in a relationship with is a 'Dr Jekyll and Mr Hyde' character – someone who is unpredictable and can be both good and evil.

The worst part about this honeymoon stage is that inevitably, because it's included in the cycle, it ends. Its ending means that the cycle is about to begin all over again.

Jeff Crippen wrote a book, *Unholy Charade – Unmasking the Domestic Abuser in the Church* (2015) and expands on Walker's original theory. He looks at The Cycle in five different stages:

The **buy-back** – The **build up** – The **set up** – The **blow up** – The **cover up.**

Crippen states that the first stage is like the honeymoon period 'the abuser is...trying to manipulatively **buy back**, through apparent peace and pleasantness, the affection and loyalty of the one he seeks to control'. The second stage, the **build up**, is where tensions increase and the perpetrator perceives everything as an attack on his authority. The third stage, the **set up**, could be seen as goading; the perpetrator is purposefully and actively setting up his victim as 'an excuse to strike'. The fourth stage, the **blow up**, is the explosion and he is focused on making sure that the victim takes the blame for his behaviour. The fifth stage, the **cover up**, overlaps with the first/honeymoon phase whereby the perpetrator appears to be sorry for what he has done and this can often seem very genuine. Crippen does note that sometimes perpetrators leave this stage out and skip back to phase one.

How can the cycle be broken?

You may be reading this having left your abuser; you have thereby already broken the cycle. You have perhaps done this alone or with friends/family and or professional help. Or you may be reading this having attempted to leave him but have gone back; or this could be the very first time you have recognised that you might be caught up in the Cycle of Abuse. Whichever part of the journey you are on, it is vital to remember that your partner's abusive behaviour is no reflection on you; it was not and is not your fault. It was him choosing to behave in a certain way and directing it at you. He could control his actions; sadly, he chose not to.

If you haven't yet left, it takes huge courage and planning to separate yourself from an abusive partner and to finally leave a Cycle of Abuse. In order for this to happen you may have to leave the family home; you may go into a refuge. You may have to leave your pets behind, you may have to change your phone number, your children may have to move schools, to name but a few changes. Women go back to a relationship numerous times before finally leaving. This is not a sign of weakness: there are so many obstacles to overcome before finally being able to leave.

However, it is important to recognise that the cycle of abuse occurs as much today as it did 40 years ago. This cycle isn't going to stop unless you are the one to stop it. This is not because you are to blame, it is because he is not going to stop. Abusers want power and control. For him to stop the cycle is for him to give up power and control and this is not in an abusive person's nature.

If you have already left your relationship you now have a list of some of the warning signs to look out for when/if you enter a new relationship. Of course, there are good men in the world, however if your next partner starts demonstrating the stages of the cycle you'll hopefully know quite quickly that you are not in a healthy relationship. Please refer to chapter 17: *Boundaries and Healthy Relationships* for more discussion on this topic.

What help is out there?

If you do decide that you are ready to break the cycle there are many options for you in terms of support.

- If you are in immediate danger you should always phone the police on 999. They are the only professionals who have the power of arrest.
- You can also phone the police on 101, which is the non-emergency number for reporting and logging information. Always ask for your crime reference number so you can log further information if necessary.
- Make a safety plan with a friend/family member and leave a small bag of your belongings at their house. See www.womensaid.org.uk/the-survivors-handbook/making-a-safety-plan/
- Speak to someone on the National Domestic Violence Helpline (0808 2000 247). They are available 24/7 and you will only ever speak to a woman. They are experienced professionals and if you would prefer to speak in your mother tongue they can organise a call with you, them and a translator.

References

Definition of cycle. (Sept 2018) Retrieved from www.merriam-webster.com/dictionary/cycle

David Finklehor, Richard J. Gelles, Gerald T. Hotaling, Murray A. Straus. (1983). **The Dark Side of Families. Current Family Violence Research**. California: SAGE Publications.

Jeff Crippen with Rebecca Davis. (2015). **Unholy Charade: Unmasking the Domestic Abuser in the Church:** Oregan, Justice Keepers Publishing.

TOP TIP
Abuse is happening during all stages of the abuse cycle, even in the honeymoon phase. The aim during this stage is to manipulate you into staying in the relationship.

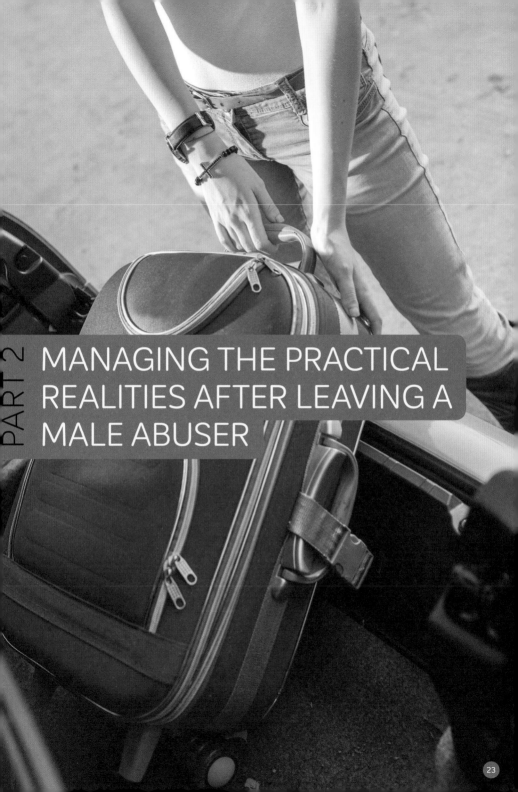

By Jan Eubanks

CHAPTER 3

Accommodation after Leaving

In this chapter, we will be exploring the range of accommodation options available to a woman after leaving an abusive relationship. Ultimately, the choice of where a woman decides to live should be her own. The place she calls 'home' often has sentimental memories and a strong attachment to it, as this may be the one place she has built a sense of identity and feels some control over. Therefore, she may find it a challenge when having to consider the safety of remaining there or moving to another accommodation.

If the abuser has left your home then one option could be to 'stay put'

Staying put
(remaining in the same accommodation).

The benefit of this option is that this is the home that you know and are comfortable in, providing you peace of mind, being near your support network and the local amenities/community links you are used to. You would not have to consider all the things needed in re-locating e.g. packing, change of GP, new tenancy/mortgage etc. If children are involved, the added considerations of nursery or school, family support and friendship ties could be maintained with minimal (if any) change.

However, it is important to acknowledge that to remain could pose continued or even potential escalation of risk, as your location is known by the perpetrator. Therefore, depending on the nature of their abusive pattern of behaviour, to stay put may expose you to the potential of targeted and increased abuse.

In order to stay, some practical considerations are needed in reviewing the level of safety of your current accommodation. A process known as 'target hardening' may be required - basically it means making it more difficult to access you or your home, eg increasing the security of all windows, doors and entry points. Some Local Authorities (LA) have contractual arrangements with local sanctuary projects to assist with this. The local community safety police or tenancy officer from either a LA or Housing Association (HA) may also be able to offer aids such as panic alarms or increased monitoring of your property/neighbourhood.

Police can consider applying special schemes (these are discretionary provisions made by some police forces on a case-by-case review), in which your address/landline is placed as an alert on a 'high-risk' list with the police. Should an emergency call be made to the police from that property, a flag is raised on their system for a speedier response to that address. Some police forces may also consider the provision of specialist mobile phones offering a similar facility, which can include tracking devices of your location and a recording facility when used in an emergency.

Beyond practical safety, it would be advisable to pay serious attention to whether you could benefit from any legal protective orders. In connection with accommodation (beyond issues around safety), the legal order known as an Occupation Order provides options around the *rights of occupancy* and use of a privately owned or rented property (including social housing). This is irrespective of who owns the property or whose name is on the tenancy agreement. Please see chapter 5 on *Legal Protective Orders*.

If the abuser still lives at the same accommodation as you and your children

Fleeing/relocating for your safety

Sometimes the risk to you/your children's safety may be so high that the safest option is to relocate. When this is the case, this reality should not be taken lightly and it is beneficial to receive a comprehensive risk assessment and support through a specialist agency. It may be necessary to flee in emergency circumstances immediately or alternatively leaving could be worked towards in a planned way. It is really important to consider a few practical things before taking the step to leave, even in an emergency. In addition to clothing,

> Sometimes the risk to you/ your children's safety may be so high that the safest option is to relocate.

toiletries, medication, etc, remember to gather important documents for you/ your children – *passports, birth certificates, medical red books, bank cards and recent statements (needed for benefit claims), driving licence and spare keys for your car,* plus special/ comfort items like toys, blankets, photos, which will help to settle you in those first few weeks when the separation from your usual home environment and loved ones may be particularly challenging. It is a good idea to have a leaving plan thought out in advance, so that you are ready to leave quickly if a chance comes up. If possible, you might be able to leave a packed bag of essential clothing, a spare phone and photocopies of important paperwork with a trusted person, ready for any emergency exit.

Have a leaving plan thought out in advance, so that you are ready to leave quickly if a chance comes up.

The UK National Domestic Violence (DV) helpline (**0808 2000 247**) is a 24 hour/365 day service co-run by Women's Aid and Refuge. (If living outside the UK check the www.hotpeachpages.net for the emergency contacts in your region). One of the services the UK DV helpline provides is help in finding availability of refuges (communal or self-contained safe houses) to any person fleeing high-risk instances of domestic abuse from a perpetrator. The Helpline offers a structured, planned and speedy process (in a lot of instances over a period of a few hours). It is important to note, though, that should a refuge be sought, it is highly likely that whatever is offered would not be located within your current local area, due to the risk from your perpetrator, and in addition could be **anywhere within the UK mainland.**

The reality of all of this could mean a big change to the environment and amenities you are used to. It could create separation and distance from family/friend networks and in most refuges there would be a strict rule about not disclosing your whereabouts to maximise your safety and reduce the chances of detection from the perpetrator and/or their associates. A more extensive step-by step guide to the process of being placed in a refuge and the common experiences and considerations in the initial weeks after being placed will be discussed in the next section.

In addition to using the National Domestic Violence Helpline, local Housing Departments and Domestic Abuse Support Services may be able to assist you, but their opening hours vary from area to area (some very limited) and thresholds for vulnerability may differ to that of the National Domestic Violence Helpline. In light of the current housing crisis, housing departments would assess vulnerability factors (beyond the risk from the perpetrator) such as if you have children, age, and any physical health/disabilities – including mental health.

In an emergency, if a LA were to assist, the most typical emergency accommodation would be provision of a B&B. This

could be for up to 33 days until a further decision is made as to whether temporary accommodation will be offered to you or if you will undergo a 'managed move' (see next section for more information). Key advice in this situation would be to utilise as many services to advocate on your behalf as possible, eg GP/health professionals, social care – if you are already in receipt of a service/ have an allocated worker, or your MP.

If you wish to flee and it's out of normal office hours, the housing department always has an on-call worker who can be contacted and can place you somewhere that night. As you are fleeing domestic violence your housing status is 'homeless'. It's worth noting that you can approach any council in the whole of the UK; it doesn't have to be your local council.

Managed Move: When needing to move but it is not an emergency

When it becomes clear that you need to move for safety reasons, a 'managed move' - with specialist services - is a good way forward. For women with either a joint or sole tenancy (whether private or social housing), local authority housing departments **always advise** that you **do not** abandon (give up your rights) to your tenancy. Even if you are seeking assistance with alternative accommodation elsewhere. Under Housing Law, to abandon a tenancy is likely to be considered making yourself and your children 'intentionally homeless'. If you were to do so, this may remove your legal right to being rehoused by the LA. It may also bring in child protection services, who could look at removing your child/ren to local authority care if they should become actually homeless. Therefore, any such moves should always be processed in consultation with a specialised domestic abuse service/housing department and in line with housing law regulations.

The benefit of a 'managed move', in conjunction with specialist services, is that the move will involve a step by step process which is not rushed. It will also allow you time to prepare emotionally for the move and practically organise other necessary requirements such as changing schools and GP, change of job/location and planning what you take with you. Many factors are involved in a managed move, eg like-for-like alternative property to swap, paying off any arrears, suitability of/preferred new location and any additional needs. This will often be time-consuming and involve several stages, which could take a few weeks or months. If you feel the need/wish to move to an alternative location, this should not dissuade you from pursuing a 'managed move'. And while this process is being completed, you may need to maximise your safety as previously described, eg target hardening, special schemes etc.

If you have a rental agreement with a private landlord and want to move, this would need to be in line with your contractual obligations, as the appropriate notice and payment of owed rent etc would be required. So this option may involve some delay and the already mentioned target hardening/alternative security measures would need to also be considered.

Entering a Refuge: Initial Stages

The first few hours

The initial moments after taking the step to flee to a refuge can be very overwhelming. There will naturally be a multitude of emotions: fear, panic, adrenaline and apprehension as to what the future may hold, and how safe you/your children will be. Common concerns may be whether you will be traced at your new location by the perpetrator, will you like the other residents/staff, will the accommodation be suitable or too different to what you are used to?

Upon arrival at the refuge, you will normally be met by at least one of the staff members. Their role will be to assist you in settling into the refuge by showing you to your room, what facilities will be solely for your use and those that may need to be shared with other residents. In all refuges you will be provided with your own room which will have basic facilities like a bed for you and bed/cot for your child/children, storage space for your clothing and personal items and sometimes your own individual fridge. You will usually share a kitchen with other residents. In some refuges, you may have an en suite but, if not, you will share a bathroom with some of the other residents. The staff member/s will devote some time to explain the structure of the refuge (staff, support offered, rules etc). There are also self-contained refuges though there are fewer of these.

During this initial entrance assessment a support worker will run through a series of questions with you. They will go through the referral sent to the refuge about your personal circumstances, the real risks posed and what your needs are. The aim is to make sure all the information recorded about you is accurate, robust in ensuring your safety but also fair in its account of your personal profile. You would then be expected to sign a tenancy agreement, which would have term & conditions included on what you can expect from the refuge but also what is expected regarding your conduct and use of the refuge.

In general, all refuges will expect that you value and work within their boundaries around safety measures. A key factor will be the expectation that you have **absolutely no contact** with the abuser throughout your stay in the refuge and that would also normally include any of his associates. **A reluctance to agree or an active decision to not abide with this rule could risk the termination of this refuge placement.** It is important for you to remember that it is **not only your safety at risk but that of other residents, their children and the staff.**

There may be an expectation not to have any contact with your close family members or friends for an interim period of time (if it could increase risk to you/your children). A risk assessment would be conducted and a clear plan made of whether any contact can take place safely and, if so, how. Understandably, this may be very hard to work with, so being honest with your support

> You will know best how comfortable you feel interacting with others at this stage.

worker about how you are or are not managing is really important to keep you focused and feeling supported. Support workers will work alongside Children's Social Services (if involved) and recommendations will be made regarding supervised contact with the other parent of your children, in another location, if it is deemed in the best interests of the child.

The range of factors addressed in your entrance assessment may well feel too much for you to take in, but is a really important opportunity for you to advise the support workers of any special needs, anxieties or questions you have. *This is your right* and you should not feel uncomfortable or embarrassed to express any questions you have. The overall benefit of going through this stage is to maximise your and your children's chances of settling in, beginning to feel accepted and embracing your new temporary home. It will also start to develop a good working partnership immediately with the support staff, where your wishes and feelings are accounted for.

During the first few hours, when moving around the refuge, you will hopefully see and be able to meet some (if not all) the residents. Again, this may well be a daunting experience. You will know best how comfortable you feel interacting with others at this stage. The exit process from your former home will have been traumatic and tiring so you may not feel up to socialising with other residents immediately. This is ok and should be understood by other residents and staff. Remember, they had 'day one' starting in the refuge just like you and will probably have felt anxious too!

Forming new friendships and a support network with the other residents is a healthy step towards rebuilding your future, but it is important to remember that building friendships naturally takes time and doesn't need to be rushed. Both you and the other residents will have had experience of abuse and may be processing difficult emotions. This may affect your/their ability to trust fellow residents and staff, the level of honesty given and how guarded you may be in being transparent and taking the risk to open up. So try to take each day one step at a time.

The first few days

The first night may seem particularly strange and long in your new home. The smells, the sounds, the shadows in the room, all will be so different to your former home and this is to be expected. You may be missing your home, your bed, home comforts, so do not be surprised if you and/or the children struggle to get a full night's sleep. To assist in settling you/the children into a refuge, wherever possible bringing a few special/comfort items, eg toys, pillow, photos can work to help reduce you missing the home you have just left.

Beyond your initial entrance assessment, a time will be arranged for you to meet again with your support worker to begin creating your support plan. This would normally include the varied roles of on-site support workers, setting out what your and your children's needs are, what goals you would like to achieve in the short-medium term and any concerns you have. The support worker would also try to begin to build into your support plan good links within the refuge, ie therapeutic 1-to-1 or group sessions and also link in with external professionals and introduce you to the local area and amenities.

1-to-1 sessions with a support worker will include practical tasks, eg budgeting, applying for benefits, transferring GP services and applying for new schools etc. In addition, you will be offered time/space to talk through how you are feeling emotionally, exploring what you feel is going well for you and your children and any issues that you may be struggling with. During every session, it would be likely that you review any safety issues arising, to ensure you remain safe whilst at the refuge. Any concerns the staff may have about your use/engagement with the refuge may also be addressed. You may also want to raise any concerns you also have and either add to or amend your support plan with any additional needs you have.

Over the next few days, you will be able to familiarise yourself with the layout and structure of how the refuge operates. In addition, conversations would be able to begin with other residents,

The first night may seem particularly strange and long in your new home.

their children and yours. It is important to again stress that there is *no obligation* to share about yourself/children with other residents. It is key that you feel comfortable and only share when you are ready to do so. This will avoid any unnecessary anxieties and sense of pressure being placed on you.

The first few weeks

Over the first few weeks, a main part of your settling in will involve you simply trying to establish basic day-to-day routines: cooking, shopping, leisure/educational activity, nursery/school attendance, medical appointments, household chores. The transition from living in your former home to communal living may be a huge change and so it would not be uncommon for you to need a bit of support in adjusting. Meeting with your support worker (normally weekly) will also continue, giving you the chance to address the areas mentioned above during the sessions.

Moving on

This will vary from resident to resident of a refuge, depending on your personal needs and also pace of recovery from the trauma experienced. It is worth noting that some refuges do have a maximum length of time you can stay so do be sure to ask this before you decide to move into refuge accommodation. Most refuges work within an *approximate* window of 6-12 months support, with the aim that during this period of time, sufficient support to you and your child/ren will have been offered and accessed. This time will also focus on settling you into the local community and process the necessary administrative/practical tasks discussed earlier in the chapter. It will also be spent processing any joint working with external agencies eg children's social care, police and working to build safety and protection plans so that when you leave the refuge you will have been empowered to regain independent living in a new community.

Notes

 TOP TIP Your safety is top priority when considering accommodation when leaving an abuser.

By Jan Eubanks

CHAPTER 4

Staying Safe: Security Measures

In addition to managing the security of your accommodation, there are other important issues to consider to maximise your safety. Whether you decide to remain in your current accommodation or move elsewhere, protecting access to your personal data is of great importance. Other points to look at are ways in which a perpetrator may attempt to continue to control your resources and level of independence, including tracking your location or activities.

Security/traceability of personal data

1) Mobile phones/computers/social media accounts

Delete your social media accounts, open new accounts in another name or restrict your access permission rights, by using the maximum privacy settings. Be aware that anyone who has access to your social media may also non-inten-

tionally share your information with your abuser or his friends/family. Therefore be vigilant and disciplined in keeping your location and activities private until such a time that you are sure everyone who sees them is a trustworthy person and not vulnerable to accidentally sharing this information. It may be worthwhile to reinforce the importance to your family/friends of their need to pay attention to this required level of security also. Keeping your location and data safe is especially important if you have children and if they have social media accounts of any kind. You may want to be aware that tracking facilities can be covertly installed by the perpetrator on your or your children's phones, tablets etc and you may want to seek advice on how to actively block or disable these from your phone/other devices.

2) Bank accounts

Open up a sole account, preferably with a different bank. Although there are now very strict rules on the collection, storage and sharing of personal information under the General Data Protection Regulation, implemented in May 2018, it is still advisable to maximise your precautionary steps. If you currently have joint accounts or credit cards, request that your name is taken off the existing account and the account be transferred solely to your ex-partner. If married or in a civil partnership, seriously consider informing the bank you are legally separated due to domestic abuse, so they do not accidentally disclose your location/personal details in situations where your account may still be/recently was linked. If you have any protective orders, e.g. a non-molestation order, it may be useful to share this with your bank to back up this request.

3) Health records

Advise your old (if there has been a change within the past year) and new GP of your safety concerns, so they can apply appropriate screening/barring of traceable information from your medical records/new location.

4) School reports/transfer of school.

This area is complex when both parents share Parental Responsibility (PR). If the perpetrator's name is on the birth certificate or he is given parental responsibility by a court, he would usually have an *automatic legal right* to be involved in his child's progress at school and access to any information on the child. Unless there is some form of order in place, ie Prohibited Steps Order or a condition within a Contact Order, where the courts have clearly ordered that information is not shared with the parent of concern, the school would be legally obliged to share information with either parent requesting information. If no legal order is in place and the abusive parent shares PR, **it is strongly recommended you seek legal advice as soon as possible** on this, if you feel this could jeopardise your or your child's ongoing wellbeing and/or safety.

5) Car registration details with DVLA/MOT test centre

Recent changes within the DVLA (2017) have opened ways in which your registered address (or at least where your car was tested) may be sourced online, as long as your name, D.O.B and vehicle registration can be verified. Due to these changes, it is essential that you notify the DVLA of any risk factors to ensure they heighten their security of your data.

6) Post Office

When leaving the relationship, it would be helpful to arrange for your post to be redirected to your new address as soon as possible. Refuges generally have a PO box address so that your location cannot be traced. When arranging the redirection of your post, advise the Post Office of your need for utmost confidentiality on your address, due to safeguarding concerns. By informing them, they can put an alert flag against your name.

7) Your employer

You may not want your employers to know of your personal circumstances but if there is any chance that risks could increase at your place of work, or disruption or interference to your emotional/professional performance, it may be helpful to at least share your situation with either your Occupational Health department and/or HR department (if not the HR manager). This is so they know the reasons behind your need for additional flexibility and/or support and possibly to avoid the risk of your competency being scrutinised under in/formal processes. The additional support they may be able to offer could include: increased security measures, eg access points to the building; counselling; time off for legal/other appointments or flexible hours/work locations. Again, if a protective order is in place, this could be shared with the relevant department at your workplace, if it feels comfortable and appropriate to do so.

Settling in after leaving an abusive relationship

Having taken the courageous step of leaving an abusive relationship, there are many different emotions that you may be going through. It is important to acknowledge that, in any relationship, attachments are made. Where you have encountered experiences of abuse/harm, there will often naturally be some degree of trauma caused. To begin the healing and recovery process from this takes time and so it is essential to be kind to yourself and accept that there will be some days that are better than others, especially in the early days after separation.

Links to support in the community

One way to help you build a successful future after leaving the relationship is to find out about services that are available locally. You may gain extra support and also reduce your chances of being isolated within the community, a key component to enhancing resilience skills for independent living and building healthy relationships in the future. These may be specialist domestic abuse agencies but could also include other support groups, focused on your needs and interests, eg interest/hobby groups, child care facilities, welfare agencies etc. By accessing a range of support agencies, you will not have to struggle alone. It can also provide an emotional network for you, to be able to speak to someone when you are not feeling so strong and also someone who may be able to empathise with your circumstances more, due to shared experiences.

If you have any additional needs, e.g. language (limited use of English/illiteracy), disability, substance misuse or

> Having taken the courageous step of leaving an abusive relationship, there are many different emotions that you may be going through.

mental health issues, accessing a specialist service will offer you a much more person-centred and holistic package of support. In addition, if you have limited use/understanding of English, or are from an ethnic minority community, engaging with specialist support groups will enable you to build more familiar and sensitive network links of support, where the group/community have a greater understanding of your needs/interests.

A note of caution here, however, with regards to cultural/religious groups. In some contexts, knowledge or close association to your personal/family network could potentially affect *(even increase*

risks to) your safety eg in honour-based, forced-marriage or modern day slavery situations. Where there is any concern of this risk, you should advise any support workers you are working with, so they are aware of such possibilities. This should include arrangements for the use of interpreters and/or accessing specific specialist community services, so as to prevent cross-connections from happening. This may be with any associates of your ex-partner/influential persons in the community. If you are not a UK citizen, it would be important to get legal advice regarding what services and support you are eligible to receive, while your status in the UK is not yet settled.

 TOP TIP Consider the security of your personal data and social and cultural links when implementing safety measures.

Notes

By Jan Eubanks

CHAPTER 5

Legal Protective Orders

The information provided on legal protective orders is purely for guidance purposes. <u>You should always seek legal advice from a qualified, independent legal representative</u>. If possible, also seek the specialist support of an Independent Domestic Violence Advocate, located in specialist domestic abuse agencies in your local area.

The most common form of protective order used, with the aim to block and stop domestic abuse behaviours by your previous partner, is referred to as an *injunction*. The role of an injunction is to prevent or prohibit the alleged abusive person (respondent) from causing consistent disruption to the victim's daily living through harmful behaviour, otherwise known as *molestation* or *harassment*. It also aims to secure the health, safety and wellbeing of the victimised person applying for the protective order (applicant) and any rel-

evant children (under 18) that the applicant cares for/lives with on a regular basis. The types of behaviours considered to be harmful are *actual or threatened violence, intimidation, pestering and harassment.* The latter can include coercive and controlling behaviours. The injunction will usually include a set of conditions:

* Not to go to a certain place (in some instances also including a defined circumference distance surrounding a set/series of locations)

- Not to display any type of behaviour that will harass and/or interrupt the named person's daily living
- Not to damage property

An injunction can be obtained either through:

A. Family Courts (civil) – victim can apply or police can apply on behalf of the victim
B. Criminal Court – police/prosecution service (CPS) apply on behalf of the victim

Family Courts

Within the family courts, there are several injunctions that can be obtained:

1) Non-Molestation Order (NMO)

This is applied for by the threatened person (the applicant) and may include any associated children (under 18) - though this is not automatically included. Under S.42 *of the Family Law Act 1996*, the family courts may issue a NMO when there are reasonable grounds to believe or evidence (current or historical) that the respondent has been violent and/or will *likely* be so in the future. This order has a Power of Arrest (POA) and, if breached, the respondent can be fined or given a maximum penalty of up to 5 years' imprisonment. A NMO *does not*, however, have the *power to evict or exclude* the respondent (abuser) if they own or have their named attached to the property where the victim also resides.

Should the victim (applicant) have additional needs and lack the capacity to represent themselves sufficiently, e.g. a learning disability or mental health needs, you have the right to appoint a *litigation friend*

(can be a friend/family member). If there is no-one you are able to appoint yourself, the courts also have the ability to appoint an *official solicitor* on your behalf.

2) Occupation Order (OO)

This order concerns *who* can occupy a property. The order includes:

a) The right to return to a property, i.e. if the victim has been evicted, excluded or temporarily fled the accommodation.
b) The right to remain within the property where there may be conflict between the applicant/respondent over who should occupy the premises. This category may have a condition attached that the respondent is requested to leave/vacate the premises.
c) If it is decided that *both parties* should/ can remain within the same dwelling, a thorough risk assessment should be made by a specialist Independent Domestic Violence Advocate, the court and, if relevant, statutory services, i.e. Social Services. Certain conditions of use can be applied, e.g. what sections of the home may be used by which party and when.
d) Even where the respondent may be listed on a tenancy agreement (whether solely/jointly) or own the premises (whether solely/jointly), an OO can demand that the respondent still contribute/cover (up to all) the rental or mortgage costs, even when they no longer reside there.
e) Positive conditions can be applied where the respondent may be required to proactively engage with support/ preventative programmes, e.g. substance misuse programme; domestic abuse preventative programme.

f) An OO can have a POA attached but this is not an automatic provision and must be requested in advance.

Both Non-Molestation Orders and Occupation Orders can be applied for with Legal Aid assistance; however, this is means-tested. This means that your daily living expenses, accessible funds, savings, employment and any equity (property, assets) will be taken into account as to whether you are eligible for Legal Aid.

3) Prohibited Steps Order (PSO)

This order is granted by the family courts, with the purpose of preventing a parent (someone who holds parental responsibility for the child/ren), *from carrying out certain actions without permission from the courts*, e.g. removal of a child/ren from a set place; taking a child/ren to certain locations etc without the explicit permission of the other parent. This order is most likely to be applied where there is concern and sufficient grounds to indicate that one parent may remove a child for a longer period of time than has been agreed or permanently, without the consent of the other parent. A PSO applies within and outside England and Wales. A breach of a PSO is a criminal matter (often referred to as *kidnapping*) and could lead to a custodial sentence.

The concerned parent can, in emergency circumstances, apply for a PSO. For the parent applying for the PSO, where there has been concern of domestic abuse, the courts would expect that parent to provide evidence to support why the other parent poses any risk of harm to the child/ren and would not act in their best interests. This could include any grounds on which you feel the parent of concern is *unfit* or *unsuitable* to be permitted such access or to be left with the child/ren. This could include factors in addition to domestic abuse, such as neglect, substance misuse, mental illness, periods of imprisonment and criminal activity etc.

A PSO is *not the same* and should not be considered equivalent to that of a Child Arrangement Order (CAO). The latter concerns decisions over where the main residence for a child will be and what contact a non-resident parent will have.

Police and criminal courts have a wide range of powers in cases of domestic abuse.

Criminal Courts

Police and criminal courts have a wide range of powers in cases of domestic abuse. In addition to the criminal laws on assault, coercive control, criminal damage, etc which may be used, there are specific orders which are designed to protect victims of domestic abuse.

1) Domestic Violence Protection Order (DVPO)*

This is a temporary form of respite order, obtained through S.24-33 of the Crime and Security Act, 2010. It is a two-stage process involving both the police and the magistrates' court. Initially the police issue a Domestic Violence Protection Notice which lasts for 48 hours. The police must then apply to the magistrates' court for a DVPO, which lasts between two and four weeks. This is usually applied for if the victim chooses not to prosecute the suspect; there is insufficient evidence for a criminal prosecution; if no bail conditions have been applied to a charge and/or where it is deemed in the best interests of the victim to set up some form of legally protective measure. Applying for a DVPO can be processed even without the victim's consent. Therefore an application for a DVPO can remove the pressure and responsibility on the victim for taking action and also affords the victim some *breathing space* to consider their options and seek specialist support from a range of professional agencies.

In order for the police to apply for a DVPO, there has to be sufficient evidence to suggest on reasonable grounds that there is a *continued risk* of the threat of/actual physical harm (which now includes severe coercive/controlling behaviours, under the *Serious Crime Act, 2015*). Once a DVPO has been awarded by the magistrates court, the conditions of prohibition on the suspect are comparable with a NMO, i.e. not contacting the victim/relevant child/ren; entering the premises where the victim resides and not approaching the premises within a set distance. In contrast to a NMO, the DVPO in addition *does have the power to evict or exclude the suspect,* even if they are living at the address, own the property or have their name attached to the property/tenancy where the victim also resides.

Once a DVPO has been granted, it becomes effective at the point it has been *served* on the suspect and a POA (Power of Arrest) is included. Although a DVPO is a civil order, *if breached,* this is a *criminal offence* and there can be a fine up to £5,000 or 2 months' imprisonment.

*The Domestic Abuse Bill (as of September 2018) proposes to change the name to a Domestic Abuse Protection Order (DAPO) and to widen its powers.

2) Restraining Order

This is obtained through the criminal courts, where a conviction has been secured or an *acquittal* or *not guilty* verdict has been reached but concerns by the professionals involved remain high. It can be used for harassment and stalking cases, and can apply to a wider range of people than just domestic violence perpetrators - their family, friends or new partner for example. The police and/or prosecution can apply for a Restraining Order to be put in place. This also has a POA attached and the same range of penalties as a NMO.

A forced marriage may be one where either one or both parties are forced into the marriage against their will.

Forced Marriage

Forced marriage is where one or both people do not consent to the marriage and they are pressured, abused or forced to do so against their will. Physical, emotional or psychological pressure might be used.

They may be taken abroad for the purpose of marriage but **do not** consent to entering into the marriage or are **unable** to reasonably give consent to the marriage. Examples of when an individual may not be able to provide informed consent could be their age and level of understanding, or having some form of impairment to their mental capacity that would impair them in competently making such a life changing decision, i.e mental health, a learning disability or being in a state of impaired cognitive consciousness (under the influence of drugs/alcohol).

It is important to note that forced marriages are illegal in the UK and constitute a criminal offence, which can incur a prison sentence of up to 7 years.

If anyone has concerns that there is risk of a forced marriage occurring, in emergency situations they should alert the police on 999. In less imminent circumstances but where concerns still exist, advice and support can be sought from the **Forced Marriage Unit**, which is a central government organisation. Furthermore, contact can also be made with either children or adult local safeguarding teams within social services.

Forced Marriage Protection Order

This can be sought by anyone, including the person being forced. They are issued through the civil courts to protect an individual considered to be at risk. This will include a list of conditions to be maintained for the individual deemed to be at risk, including that they must not be removed from the country and/or have pressure applied on them to enter into a marriage. The breach of a forced marriage protection order (*which is a civil order, like with DVPN/O's*) is also a criminal offence and can lead to up to a 5 year custodial sentence even if the marriage does not take place.

Notes

 TOP TIP Get professional legal advice and professional domestic abuse support when seeking a protective order.

Sources of further information and support:
- 24 hour National Domestic Violence Helpline – 0808 200 0247
- Women's Aid (IDVA) - https://www.womensaid.org.uk/
- Rights of Women (free legal advice by phone) - http://rightsofwomen.org.uk/
- Law Society (find a solicitor) – 020 7320 5650 – www.solicitors.lawsociety.org.uk
- Legal Aid Agency – 0345 345 4 345
- Court forms and locations – www.justice.gov.uk/about/hmcts
- Forced Marriage Unit Helpline – 0207 008 0151

By Jan Eubanks

CHAPTER 6

No Contact, Co-Parenting or Parallel Parenting?

The issue of whether to remain in contact with your abuser once you have exited an abusive relationship can be an extremely difficult and emotive decision to make; especially when you have children together. The balance between protecting your own emotional welfare and safety, whilst organising shared custody, is not an easy goal to achieve. The key to remember is that you <u>are</u> a survivor of harmful abuse and have demonstrated much courage and resilience to reach the position you are now in! Therefore it is important that your plans and decisions for the future maintain a sense of _self-worth, independence and autonomy._

Due to an individual's beliefs, there can sometimes be pressure from members of your community and friends to either reconcile or remain on 'friendly' terms with your abusive ex-partner. Remember, however, that it is **not ever** the right or responsibility of any family member, friend or religious leader to place undue pressure or obligation on you as to what decisions you make around contact/parenting options. It can be very easy and tempting at times for others, outside your home situation and individual experience of abuse, to express their personal/religious beliefs, sometimes also imposing value judgements on what decisions you should make. Despite this, do not fear being set free from this pressure and continually embrace Romans 8:1 - which reminds us that:

Therefore, there is now no condemnation for those who are in Christ Jesus.

In this new stage of your life, you are moving to a place of emotional, physical, spiritual and cognitive restoration. You are healing and rebuilding the *core* of your self-esteem that has likely been chipped away through the abuse that you've experienced. Therefore, God is the only person who should redefine your identity and self-worth in Christ. Furthermore, it has never been, nor ever will be, God's intention that you live a life of continual bondage through being a victim of ongoing abuse. Rather, His desire and ultimate plan is that you would exist in a *strong, healthy and positive state* in the freedom that He provides. As Galatians 5:1 says:

It is for freedom that Christ has set us free. Stand firm, then, and do not let yourselves be burdened again by a yoke of slavery.

In recognition of this, your total validation and freedom is in Christ alone and no-one else! He is the author and perfecter of your faith, in regard to every decision you make in your day to day life. You no longer have to be subjected to or accept any form of manipulation, coercion, judgement or intimidation.

No Contact

A number of considerations need to be taken into account when reaching your decision as to whether to continue to engage with your abuser. If you have no children, most specialist professionals advocate, where there has been either a significant one-off incident and/or the presence of systematic and continued abuse, that **no contact** whatsoever be engaged in after leaving your abuser. **No contact**, in its purest sense, means **'no'** contact. Therefore, **no** responding to telephone calls, **no** email exchanges, **no** social media contact, **no** letters or messages conveyed through other people. This involves both direct contact to yourself (in person or indirectly) or via friends/family.

If children are involved, you may have to engage in some form of shared parenting (even if not your preferred choice) should the abuser apply to family court and successfully be awarded shared residency/contact. There are two different theoretical approaches to shared parenting: *Co-Parenting* or *Parallel Parenting*.

Co-Parenting

This approach includes the inherent belief that an *amicable* context of shared parenting is always in the best interest of the child/ren. It also hopes that, between both parents, there will be a mutual degree of respect in how each parent makes decisions and sets bound-

> In this new stage of your life, you are moving to a place of emotional, physical, spiritual and cognitive restoration.

aries. This relates to the child/ren when in either parent's care but also when joint decisions may be required. This style of shared parenting is promoted on the basis of *developing co-operation* between both parents. It strives to demonstrate to the child/ren that a degree of partnership and respect for the other parent can still be achieved, irrespective of the breakdown of their relationship.

There is strong caution regarding this theoretical perspective on *co-parenting* by many abuse specialists, because this approach requires a high degree of mutual respect, trust, co-operation and 'letting go of control'; which many could argue an abuser is far less likely to be able to honestly and willingly engage in. So this is **not** often a viable parenting approach when leaving an abuser, based upon the history and foundation of the imbalance of power in the former relationship.

Some examples of the divisive and manipulative tactics that the abusive partner may try to engage in when involved in co-parenting are:

- excessive inquiring, surveillance and micro-managing your and/or the child/ren's personal routines and social activities.
- overindulgence in the provision of known prohibited items, being presented as gifts for the children and/or yourself, which the abusive parent is aware will cause confusion and/or tension when the children return home - 'playing mind games'.
- negative, threatening or divisive comments being made in front of the children during contact sessions,

in respect of yourself as the other parent, your family members and/or new partner, the aim being to cause conflict in your home/during your time of caring for the child/ren.
- Using real (or false) accounts of ill-health or misfortune in their circumstances, e.g. loss of job/ bereavement, to make you pay more time, attention and have pity on them; with the aim of encouraging you to 'let your guard down' and/or be more accommodating to their needs.
- indirectly sending messages back to the survivor parent, on how the abusive parent expects the home life for the mother and child/ren *should* be and how decisions *should* be made; ultimately continuing to inflict some degree of *control* from a distance.
- intentional defiance, disruptive and/ or evasive responses to specific decisions being made with respect to the children or promoting opposing routines, to those which you are working hard to maintain within your home, e.g. types of food, access to gadgets or bedtimes. These behaviours are known as 'counter-parenting'.

Be aware, however, that such manipulative behaviour is not solely manifested in a negative manner. Equally the abusive parent may subtly use a *calculated and systematic flow of positive and accommodating behaviours*. This can be in the form of:

- gifts towards yourself and the children - in this instance to impress, woo and emotionally 'draw you back' to your abusive ex.
- expressions of remorse, emotional distress and reassurances that they are

a 'changed man', e.g. tears in front of the children - again with the primary intention to confuse and woo you and/or the children back and soften you to the possibility for reconciliation.

- *exceptionally* reasonable or charming behaviours.

The motivation and intention of being exceptionally reasonable and charming is also a power tool and tactic to regain control over you and should be *just as much* of a warning sign for you to be cautious and mindful when the abusive parent uses the *'Prince Charming'* strategy.

Parallel Parenting

By establishing a more robust and formalised position with regard to boundaries and safeguards, some professionals advocate that a more independent/ detached style of shared parenting can be achieved after leaving your abuser. This is through what is known as *Parallel Parenting*.

This approach emphasises the reality that, in a situation where control and coercion have been systematically enforced upon you, it may well be an unrealistic and unfeasible goal to ever seek amicable shared parenting that includes an equal balance of power. With this in mind, advocates for this approach would suggest there is absolutely no point in attempting co-parenting and that it *could actually be very damaging to you and the children* by continuously devoting your energy and efforts trying to achieve this non-realistic objective. In contrast, when adopting

the parallel parenting approach, you are encouraged to decide on what *key aspects* of raising your children require communication and what decisions need to be made mutually, between both parents. *Only for these areas* of the child/ren's upbringing would you make contact and, even then, you would focus on establishing very clear and robust boundaries around the amount and manner of contact you have with the abusive parent. This might be through email, using a "parent communication notebook" or a "parenting meeting" with a neutral third party (always) present.

This approach involves a *disciplined* strategy and *determination* to no longer fight with or against the abusive parent, in respect of minor decisions towards the care and upbringing of your child/ren, e.g. food, access to gadgets etc unless, for medical/other grounds, serious harm could be caused by overlooking these issues. It is also important to remember that you are under **no** obligation to endure further emotional or other abuse because *'you are a Christian'* or *'for the sake of the children'*. This pressure is unhelpful and can be harmful. Avoid accepting responsibility for the abuser's actions and be assertive in laying the responsibility of his harmful behaviours (back) in his hands.

When engaging in parallel parenting, it is *essential* that you create a very clear *separation* and *space* between you and the other parent. Ultimately, you are seeking to *reduce and eliminate* any form of con-

> Ultimately, you are seeking to reduce and eliminate any form of conflict with the other parent.

flict with the other parent. This will always be in the best interest of you and your child/ren's well-being. Very firm boundaries around limited contact between yourself and the other parent could include:

1. The mode through which you expect to correspond with the other parent, e.g. email, text, through a 3rd party. This will offer you some degree of *space* and *choice* as to what you want to respond to and also avoid spontaneously being drawn into unnecessary and unhealthy conflict - more likely in a telephone conversation. If need be, at a later stage, should any continued pattern of harassment or abuse arise, texts/emails can provide a source of evidence.

2. In most instances there will rarely be any reason why you should have direct contact by phone (conversations) or in person. Therefore serious consideration should be made as to completely blocking any form of direct (spoken) telephone communication or in person between yourself and your ex-partner. It is your right and choice to say that you do not want this form of contact. Even when you use text or email communication, it should be strictly limited to arranging and discussing logistical decisions e.g. collection and drop off times/points, proposed activities and appointments e.g. medical. You may wish to set up a completely separate email/mobile phone account (if you can afford this) *solely* for communication with the other parent, being disciplined to only access this at set times and for this one reason only.

Also, where there may be a Non-Molestation Order or Restraining Order already in

place, these conditions around methods of contact may already be ordered by the courts (or you could consider requesting these conditions to be included as part of your initial application).

3. Ensure that any professional agencies involved such as schools, GP's, health services, family courts are *made aware* of your requirement to limit the communication and the release of data to your ex-partner. This will include making them aware of any active protective orders in place, to legally enforce your rights and wishes in protecting your private and personal data being released and or removing their status as next of kin/spouse (if legally separated/divorced). In addition, the respective agency would then be empowered to be mindful of any conflict of interests and risks; hopefully increasing the likelihood of making more appropriate responses, with balanced and impartial decisions to safeguard and act in the best interests of yourself and your child/ren.

Be mindful and be aware, where the other parent holds legal parental responsibility (whether they play an active role in the child/ren's life or not) they have legal rights of access and involvement in your child/ren's care. So unless *you* advise such agencies of any legal protective orders in place, the professional agency will be legally and *mutually obliged* upon request from the other parent to release information about your child. So it is in *your and your children's interests* to inform any agency of any potential safeguarding risks posed to you.

4. Do not be intimidated by further threats and/or acts of intimidation. This may include threats around withdrawal of child support/maintenance, entering into further legal proceedings or the

involvement of Children's Social care, police etc. Clearly outline your conditions for communication and that you **will not** tolerate such behaviours. Should this be ignored and persisted in, you may want to indicate that you will need to terminate all forms of informal communication and thereafter communicate through a legal representative. Often (but not always) you will find the reality of your abusive ex being required to spend further money, to solely communicate with you through a solicitor can often act as an effective deterrent. Thereafter, do not respond to this intimidation and if required, seek legal advice and proceed with the most appropriate approach in reporting such concerns and prohibiting this behaviour.

5. Avoid any joint child-related events wherever possible. Family, friends, church leaders/ members and even professional agencies i.e Children's Social Care *should* not *but may try to* place a degree of pressure on you, to jointly attend an event in the immediate presence of your ex-partner. Where your presence and input is required, careful planning should provide you with the opportunity to accommodate your attendance but at a separate time and possibly a separate day to the other parent eg school parents evening; child protection case conferences.

6. Filter and minimise the attention and responses paid to your ex, when concerning your children. Learn to *'let go'* and only respond to the things that cause serious harm to your child/ren. When engaged

in parallel parenting, it is likely that there will be occasions that you disagree with the choices and style of parenting of the other parent. However, it is essential that you keep hold of the fact that you have decided to move away and actively *detach* yourself from the emotional connection to your ex-partner. Significant gains from this process of detachment include: building strength and resilience skills in *not allowing the less harmful* activities or the lifestyle conducted in the other parent's home to play an intrusive part in your life e.g. different bedtimes, activities, less nutritious choice of foods (unless causing direct harm/adding to a pre-existing health concern).

Although the differences in arrangements within both households may irritate you, *a significant part of your liberation and healing is to try to ignore and not hold on to these differences.* On a positive note, children are very versatile and resilient and can adapt to variable environments e.g. from home to school, where rules and boundaries may differ at times. Should your child mention to you any concerns they have about the other home environment, encourage that child to build the confidence to speak directly to the other parent (if feasible and where the other parent is likely to be willing to listen and acknowledge your child/ ren's needs). Enabling your child/ren to express their wishes and concerns directly to the other parent (and/or this parent's extended family/support network), can create a distance and protection for yourself, in not being drawn in to any further

> On a positive note, children are very versatile and resilient and can adapt to variable environments.

conflict with the other parent. It can also develop skill and resilience in your child/ren, to be empowered to communicate directly with their other parent and not feeling that they always have to be rescued by you. This strategy also avoids the potential of the 'good cop, bad cop' dynamic from divisively developing, which could further increase the potential of conflict between both parents. Nevertheless, if there is a very serious concern, you may need to raise it with the other parent (through safe means) and if not dealt with appropriately, you may need to seek professional help or action through the courts and/or children's social care.

The overall idea of parallel parenting is that *you **retain control, dignity and choice over how you parent your children***, establishing firm *boundaries* and *distance* from your abusive ex. It also removes your child/ren from being in the middle of any conflict. Ultimately, you **empower yourself and your children** and increase your chances of achieving good outcomes and an enhanced quality of life in the future.

If local safeguarding teams (within social services) consider your child/ren and/or yourself to be at risk, they may have a legal duty to intervene and may therefore make certain requirements of you (as the main/shared carer) regarding the level of contact or other requirements. As far as is possible and deemed reasonable, aim to work in partnership with the local safeguarding teams. However, if any serious concerns arise, know that it is your right to seek independent legal advice to review/challenge their recommendations. Their role is to act in the *best* interests of the child/ren and their paramount **duty** is to protect your child/ren from 'significant harm' – Children Act, 1989; S.47.

Now that you have left your abuser, you have the space, freedom and autonomy to make decisions for you and your children's future life. **Be empowered to enjoy this space and freedom**. Finally, make **safe and wise** decisions, keeping in balance your overall psychological and physical wellbeing and safety.

TOP TIP Your decisions regarding contact should always ensure your safety, sanity and dignity. Seek to maintain a sense of self-worth, independence and autonomy.

Notes

By Louisa Whitney

CHAPTER 7

The Divorce Process and Financial Considerations

The family justice system in England and Wales is complicated and it can seem difficult to understand. The aim of this chapter is to give you a summary of how it works so that you have information about the different parts involved. I also want to help you to know where to find the support you need. This can make all the difference. The system aims to protect those who need it and to ensure fairness is achieved. Separating from a partner is one of the most stressful life events and is sometimes likened to a bereavement, as you lose the life you thought you would have. It can be compounded by other issues like domestic abuse. I use this term in this chapter to include violence – or threats of violence, emotional abuse such as constantly saying hurtful things or controlling someone by not letting them have money or preventing them from keeping in touch with friends or family. It can take time to heal from these wounds but with a little knowledge and the right help you can find an outcome that will mean you can start the next chapter of your life.

The Divorce Process

The divorce process is about legally ending your marriage. *It doesn't automatically deal with any other related issues such as child residency or finances.* You have to deal with these separately, however these issues are usually resolved at the same time as the divorce. Despite all the talk in the newspapers about 'quickie' celebrity divorces, the divorce process takes the same time for everyone. It depends how quickly everyone deals with paperwork, but a divorce can be achieved in 6 months from start to finish (and sometimes a bit less). The time is extended where there are problems with paperwork, or where there are issues about money that have not been resolved. It is possible to end the divorce process without sorting out money issues but you would usually be advised that sorting out money issues is best before applying for the last part of your divorce.

You can only petition for a divorce if your marriage is definitely at an end (most people wouldn't do this unless it was anyway!) You have to show that your marriage is over by using one of five different facts. These are adultery, unreasonable behaviour, separation for 2 years (where the other person agrees to this), separation for 5 years (where the other person doesn't have to agree), or desertion (where the other person left intending not to return and has been gone for 2 years). Be aware that if you are petitioning for divorce on the basis that you have been separated for two years, the other person needs to agree to this and

they may not agree, or they may try to put conditions on their agreement. If you feel that this behaviour is a possibility then it may be sensible to petition for divorce on a different basis. You should also be aware that if you apply on the basis of their adultery, then if they dispute this you may be asked to provide evidence of the adultery. If this is a battle you would rather not have, then applying on the basis of the other person's unreasonable behaviour can be a better way forward. The test for unreasonable behaviour is only what is unreasonable to you and not to anybody else. You are not required to prove the unreasonable behaviour.

The test for unreasonable behaviour is only what is unreasonable to you.

You start a divorce by sending a divorce petition to the court together with your marriage certificate (you can get a copy if you don't have the original). You also need to pay the fee or fill out a form to exempt you from the fee and provide the supporting evidence that you are on benefits or on a low income (the form explains this in more detail). I should point out that a lawyer can do all the paperwork for you if you qualify for legal aid, or if you instruct them on a paying basis to do so. Legal aid is not widely available now for advice about family matters, but it is for victims of domestic abuse.

Once you have sent your petition to the court, the court sends it to the other person together with a form that they need to complete to acknowledge that they have received the divorce petition. If they do not do this then you have to show the court that they have definitely received it. This can either be done by providing proof they have received it, e.g. a text message where they talk about this, or by asking the court bailiff to give them the petition in person. There are special procedures and forms for each stage which a lawyer can talk you through, or you can find the forms online and each form has notes on how to complete it.

Once you have shown the court that the other person has got the divorce petition, you can then apply for the next stage. This is asking the court to grant a Decree Nisi which is the middle stage of the divorce. This is spoken out loud by a judge in court but you do not need to go to court to hear this being done. Six weeks from the day after this happens, you can apply for the final stage of the divorce which is called the Decree Absolute. Once the Decree Absolute is granted, you are divorced. If there are unresolved money issues, then it may be sensible not to apply for this final stage until they are sorted out. This is because if the other person died before you had resolved issues about money then you may be left in a financially vulnerable position because you may lose your rights to inherit certain financial benefits on their death – for example if they have a pension.

> **If there are unresolved money issues, then it may be sensible not to apply for this final stage until they are sorted out.**

It is possible for the other person to defend the divorce petition, which means they argue to the court that the divorce should not be given, or that they can start their own petition based on one of the 5 facts I have explained above. Such a step is unusual because most lawyers would advise against it as it doesn't change the end result of getting divorced and takes up more time, cost and effort. In the main, it is something people may threaten but it happens infrequently in practice.

Issues about money
Leaving a marriage can present some real financial difficulties – especially if you did not work or are on a low income, and even more so if you are leaving an abuser who controlled money (and may continue to do so). If you are struggling to make ends meet, then it's important to get help with money so that you are at least able to find somewhere to live and to pay bills and buy food. Please refer to chapter 9: *Managing your Money:Budgeting* and chapter 10: *Dealing with Debt*. In addition, your local Citizens Advice Bureau (CAB) will often have someone who understands benefits, who can advise you about what you might be entitled to. You can find your nearest CAB by looking at *www.citizensadvice.org.uk/ about-us/how-we-provide-advice/advice/search-for-your-local-citizens-advice/*

There is also information about benefits on the *gov.uk* website. You can apply for maintenance for a child through the Child Maintenance Enforcement Commission (which used to be called the Child Support Agency or CSA) but you need to speak to this service first www.cmoptions.org. If you are a victim of domestic abuse then you may not have to pay the normal fee

to use this service. Children's Sure Start Centres sometimes have people to assist with this too. There are also now many local food banks that you can find by searching online (which you can do at your local library if you don't have access to the internet at home). If you have a lawyer and are eligible for Legal Aid, then you may be able to make an application for money from your ex-partner to tide you over until money issues between you are sorted out on a long term basis. You can also approach your local authority about housing – again an online search of your local area should tell you who to contact.

If there are issues about money such as a property, savings or other assets (like pensions, shares or investments), then you will need to address these. Be aware that where you have been married you may be entitled to a share in any money the other person has, regardless of whether you have contributed to this or not. It's important that you get advice

about this from a professional and that you do not simply accept what the other person says about this. They may want to keep all the money for themselves and to avoid sharing any of it with you. You may also be entitled to more money each month for yourself, on top of any money paid to you for the benefit of a child. It will depend on what the other person earns, and what their monthly bills are. This is called spousal maintenance. It is only available where you have been married to the partner you're separating from. It is impossible to say here what money a person would be entitled to because the law in this area is complicated and depends on each individual couple's circumstances. But the court will always want to ensure that both parties to the marriage are able to house themselves and to make ends meet (i.e. to pay their bills and to afford to feed themselves). There are various factors that are taken into account in deciding what is a fair outcome with regard to separating a couple's money and these are:

- The money you have (whatever form it is in) and what ability you have to earn money. This might include your qualifications but might also include things that affect how much you can work like having the care of young children.
- The financial needs each of you has and what you have to pay out, for example in housing costs, or to support dependent children.
- The standard of living you had during the marriage – did you drive nice cars and go on lots of holidays or did you struggle to make ends meet even when you lived together?
- How old each of you are and how long you were married to each other.
- Any physical or mental ill health or disability either of you has.
- The contributions you each made, which might include the money that you've earned but may also include looking after children and the home so that the other person could go out to work. This contribution is considered to be a equally as important as working and earning money.
- The behaviour of each of you - which might include behaviour that has caused financial hardship to either or both of you, or bad behaviour such as a criminal offence having been committed that has affected either of you.
- Where either of you would be financially worse off just because of the divorce, e.g. if you received money from a family trust that only paid an income to you whilst you were married.

If you have been a victim of domestic abuse, then it's important to get help from a lawyer who understands the issues you may be facing. When making contact with lawyers, ask whether they regularly deal with cases involving domestic abuse. It is important that you find someone who you feel can help you, and there is nothing wrong with telephoning a few different law firms to find someone who you think understands your situation, before making an appointment. You can find a domestic abuse specialist by searching Resolution's website via this link www.resolution.org.uk/find_a_specialist/. Resolution is an organisation that represents lawyers (and other professionals such as mediators and IFAs) who work with couples who separate. All members subscribe to their code of conduct, which puts children's needs first in resolving issues. You can also search all lawyers by searching for a lawyer on the Law Society's website *www.lawsociety.org.uk.* You can search for someone who specialises in family issues on this website but, unfortunately, not someone who is a domestic abuse expert. You can also take a friend, family member or support worker to an initial meeting with a lawyer to support you and to assist you in remembering information. It is helpful if the support person can take a notebook and pen to note down key pieces of information for you – and any next steps that it is suggested you should take.

You may be eligible for legal aid which will pay for your legal advice (which will include completing court forms) if you

If you have been a victim of domestic abuse then it's important to get help from a lawyer that understands the issues you may be facing.

have been a victim of domestic abuse, and are reliant on a low income, or benefits. You can find out by visiting www.gov.uk/check-legal-aid. If you do qualify then you need to find a lawyer who offers legal aid. You can do a search for lawyers near you who specialise in family matters and offer legal aid through the website searches set out above.

To resolve issues concerning money there are different processes that you can use and these are:

1) Mediation

This involves you and the other person coming to the same place to talk about the issues that need to be resolved, with the benefit of an independent and impartial professional family mediator. You can be in separate rooms, or it can take place online if you are worried about being in the same place as the other person. There is now a big emphasis on mediation and it is compulsory to try mediation before applying to the court, except in certain circumstances. If you have been a victim of domestic abuse then you may be exempt from the need to try mediation before starting a court application. It is up to you whether you feel strong enough and able to try mediation. If it is something you are interested in then you can talk to a family mediator about this. There will always be an initial assessment meeting that should take place separately from the other person and you can discuss any concerns you have with the mediator. Legal

aid is available for family mediation so, if this is an option you would like to pursue, you can search for a family mediator who offers legal aid via Resolution's website or the Family Mediation Council *www.family-mediationcouncil.org.uk*. You can also find a suitable local non-legal aid family mediator using these search facilities if you wish to. Do check with the mediator that they offer legal aid if you are eligible, as the search facility for this is not always reliable.

The mediator has to make a judgement about whether mediation is suitable in your case. It can often be the quickest and most cost-effective way of resolving matters, but it is not appropriate for everyone and it would not be appropriate if it would cause you to fear for your personal safety or to be severely anxious, or if the other person would try to manipulate you through this process. If you are concerned about this then it is necessary to have some safeguards in place, e.g. attending mediation in a separate room from your ex-partner or establishing clear ground rules beforehand. If you feel that mediation is being used as a way to renew or prolong an abusive relationship, then it's important that you indicate this and draw it to a close.

> If you feel that mediation is being used as a way to renew or prolong an abusive relationship then it's important that you indicate this and draw it to a close.

2) Collaborative Practice

This is a bit like mediation as issues are discussed by sitting together in the same room, but with each party having a specially trained collaborative lawyer rather than one mediator. The emphasis is on being constructive, with the needs of children at the top of the agenda. Everybody involved, including the lawyers, agrees that you won't apply to the court. Where there has been domestic abuse this may not be an appropriate process to use. You can chat to a collaboratively trained family lawyer if you would like to learn more about this process. You can find such a lawyer through Resolution's website.

3) Negotiating

Directly with each other or through lawyers. Where you negotiate through lawyers this tends to involve lawyers writing to each other on your behalf rather than talking round a table (although it is possible to do this). If you have discussed matters with each other directly and come to an agreement, it's crucial that this is properly drawn up by lawyers to ensure that you each have to stick to what you have talked about (this is true no matter which process you use).

4) The court process

This is the only process that can force someone to talk about issues, or order them to do things they don't want to do, such as giving you information about their financial situation. It is a crucial part of any process that you each provide financial information to each other so that you both properly understand what money you have. You have to complete an application form to ask the court to deal with your money issues and pay a fee (unless you are on benefits or a low income). For the last few years there has been a rule that you try mediation before you apply to the court but you may be exempted from this if you have been a victim of domestic

abuse. The form explains what the exclusions are and how you can give proof of this (There are a number of ways so don't worry about this).

5) Arbitration

This is like court in that another qualified person makes decisions about what should happen next. But it's a bit like having an operation privately rather than on the NHS. You can choose which arbitrator you use (the court will give you a judge on the day and you have no choice about this). The court process is the same for everyone, regardless of how much money they have. By using arbitration you can make the process work for you by cutting out the bits of the court process that are unnecessary – for example if you only have a house and a small income you probably don't need to complete a 30 page form about your money situation. Arbitration is not compulsory. It needs both people to agree to it for it to happen.

This website explains more about the different processes: *www.resolution.org.uk/landing-two-cols.asp?page_id=1174*

In the next chapter we will look at issues relating to your children and how to seek protection for yourself if you are concerned for your own (or your children's) safety. I also explain how to get help to address these issues.

TOP TIP

Where you have been married, you may be entitled to a share in any money the other person has, regardless of whether you have contributed to this or not. The court will always want to ensure that both parties to the marriage are able to house themselves and to make ends meet.

Notes

By Louisa Whitney

CHAPTER 8

The Divorce Process and Children

As well as the legal ending of a marriage and sorting out issues about money, there may also be concerns and issues surrounding your children and your own (and possibly your children's) protection. The purpose of this chapter is to outline the steps that you can take if you feel that your children have been affected by your separation, or by things that may have happened during the marriage (or relationship). It's also designed to deal with scenarios where you can't agree who your children should live with. It also outlines what steps you can take if you feel you need protection from your ex-partner. Again this chapter is written to help you have a basic understanding of 'the system' and to look at how you can find any help that you need.

Child Living Arrangements

Separation raises issues as to when children should live with one parent and when they should live with the other parent. There are no rules about this in any law and it is ideally the responsibility of the parents to come up with an arrangement that will work for everyone involved. It is crucial that, as part of any separation, children understand that they are loved by both parents, that they are free to have a relationship with both parents, and that none of what has happened is their fault. All of the studies that have been done point to the fact that separation is not what causes harm, it is being exposed to conflict between their parents (and remember, most children see themselves as being 50% of one parent and 50% of the other).

This question of when children see each parent is a more difficult one where there has been an abusive relationship. If you have concerns about your ex-partner causing any harm (be it physical or emotional) to the children but he wants the children to live with him also, then you may need to get professionals involved. Professionals will help guide the children's living arrangements by working with your family.

All of the studies that have been done point to the fact that separation is not what causes harm, it is being exposed to conflict between their parents.

Where there is no suggestion of the children being harmed but you are fearful of seeing your ex partner, you can look at whether a friend or family member could take the children to and from their father to prevent you having to see him.

This is a tough thing to sort out. You may have been badly affected by your ex-partner's behaviour and your natural instinct is to want to remove your children from something that has been particularly harrowing for you. It is important to look at your children's experience of the same relationship and whether they too have been exposed to forms of abuse, or whether they have experienced the other person as a largely loving parent in spite of his actions towards you. It is an incredibly hard thing to do to look at someone who has caused you so much angst and hurt and to see them through somebody else's eyes. Courts are always keen to ensure that children have a relationship with both parents, unless it would cause the children harm to do this. It's also important to remember that it doesn't have to be all or nothing. If the other parent is in agreement, you can look at an arrangement where the children see the other parent for a short period of time initially (in a safe and supported environment) and you then look to build this up by reviewing it every few months, to see how everybody feels the arrangement is working. Again, if you are accessing support as a family then you can ask professionals, who know your family, for guidance with these difficult issues.

Ultimately, it is up to you and the other parent to put in place arrangements for your children when you separate. You can use any of the processes set out in the chapter about divorce and money issues (mediation, collaborative practice, negotiating, arbitration or court proceedings) to resolve issues concerning your children. No agency will interfere with arrangements you both agree to, provided that your children are safe from any form of harm. Where there is concern about your children being harmed then you (or another agency) may need to take steps to ensure your children are safe. Court proceedings are the only process that can force issues and offer you protection in an emergency. For example, if you are worried about the other parent taking your children away from you, or leaving the country with them, then you may need to urgently ask the court to make an order preventing them. As with the divorce and financial issues, you can use a lawyer to apply to the court but you can also apply yourself by completing an application form that you can find on the court's website *www.gov.uk/government/organisations/ hm-courts-and-tribunals-service.*

If you want the court to deal with issues concerning your children, then there is a rule that you try mediation before you apply to the court (as I outlined in the chapter concerning divorce and money matters) but you would be excluded from this where there has been domestic abuse, or where you need help or protection urgently. Again if you qualify for legal aid, then a lawyer would be able to help you with making the application without you having to pay. A court will only get involved in arrangements for a child where the child needs protection from harm, or where the child's parents are unable to agree on arrangements for that child (or children). This might include circumstances where you are unable to agree which parent your children should live with, or how often they should see or live with the other parent. Courts used to talk about "custody" and "access" but these are very emotive terms and so haven't been used for nearly 30 years. The phrases used now are "residence" and "contact", made under a "Child Arrangements Order", because the court will make arrangements for your

children if their parents are unable to make arrangements themselves (either because they cannot agree between them what is right for their children, or for some other reason).

It's important to recognise that the other parent may want your children to be with them more than you feel is appropriate. They then have the right to ask the court to decide this if you do not agree. This can be a stressful experience – especially so where you have left an abusive partner. The court will focus on what is best for the children and may not be too concerned with the abuse where it is considered to be of a low level. This can be upsetting and frustrating.

CAFCASS (The Children and Family Court Advisory and Support Service), social workers who work for the court, usually become involved when one parent asks the court to deal with an issue concerning a child. They will meet with both parents and the child or children and get information from other agencies like social services, your children's schools and sometimes the police (if they have been involved) to form a view of what is best for your children. They act as the court's 'eyes and ears' in the family so that they can tell the court about your children's wishes and feelings. They do this in the form of a written report but may also be asked to attend court to explain more about their conclusions to the judge. They can explain what the children would like to happen and what, in their professional opinion, is best for them. Their website also has some useful information that may help you: www.cafcass.gov.uk/grown-ups/parents-and-carers/resources-parents-carers/.

It's important that you share any concerns you have with the CAFCASS officer so that they can form a full picture. A judge will usually be guided by the CAFCASS report, as this is written by an expert in dealing with children, but they are not obliged to be, and there are circumstances in which they won't follow all of the report's recommendations. You

may then be left in a situation where your children spend more time or live with your ex-partner more than you would like, this can be a difficult situation to manage as you may feel that you are being required to engage with your abuser more than you want. Having a book that is shared between you and your ex-partner to write things in concerning the children can be a useful way of minimising interaction between the two of you when the children are collected or dropped off. This can be used for important information concerning the children such as recording any medication they have had or may need, any items they need to remember to come back with, details of any homework that needs doing, or information about their welfare, such as whether they got upset or hurt themselves. You may also choose to communicate only via email or text with your ex partner so that telephone calls or face to face meetings are not needed. Please refer to chapter 6: *No Contact, Co-Parenting vs Parallel Parenting* for more information.

Protecting You and Your Children

If you (or your children) have been a victim of any form of abuse and you feel you need protection from your ex-partner then you can, in an emergency, dial 999 to obtain assistance from the police. You can also report incidents to the police after the event, even if you are unable or unwilling to dial 999 at the time. Physical violence and threats of violence are a criminal offence. There is also now a new

If you (or your children) have been a victim of any form of abuse and you feel you need protection from your ex partner then you can in an emergency dial 999 to obtain assistance from the police.

criminal offence of coercive behaviour, which may offer you protection against other behaviours. If your ex-partner is charged with an offence, then it can be a condition of them being allowed to leave the police station (called bail) that they do not come and talk to you or get in touch with you.

You, or your children, can also seek protection through the court by obtaining a Non-Molestation Order and an Occupation Order (often referred to as an injunction). A Non-Molestation Order is an order that says the other person must not hurt you (or your children) or threaten you or get anyone else to do this on their behalf. Doing anything that breaks this order is a criminal offence for which they can be arrested and prosecuted. An Occupation Order is an order that you are able to stay in a particular place (which may be your current home) and your ex-partner is ordered to leave that property and not to go within a set distance of it. Again, if they break this they can be arrested and charged. The court can also order that they continue to pay the rent or mortgage on the property they are leaving, to ensure that you are able to stay there.

A specialist lawyer can help you to obtain these orders (using legal aid if you are eligible) or you can apply yourself directly to the court using the online forms on the court's website, which is included above. Domestic abuse charities may be able to support you in making these applications too. The police often pass victims details of local support organisations, and making contact with your local organisation can be a good way of getting support.

If you are being subjected to physical harm, threats of physical harm, constant insults, money being withheld from you, or you are prevented from reaching out to the police or friends or family (or are experiencing any other behaviour that makes you feel deeply uncomfortable, anxious or fearful), then it is a good idea to keep a written log of any incidents of abusive behaviour that are directed at you (or your children or other family members or friends trying to help) so that you can be clear about what happened and when. This will help you if you ask the police or the courts for help in protecting you (and your children). Also, if you log all incidents with the police by reporting them, then this can help the police to build up a picture of what is happening, which then means they are able to take action even where they may not have been able to after one incident.

> Giving children the space to be able to talk to you and to express how they're feeling can be helpful.

Where you apply to the court for protection by way of a Non-Molestation and/or an Occupation Order, you are more likely to persuade a judge to make this order if you are able to be clear about incidents that have happened, and give clear details about what has happened and when. If you are able to keep threatening or abusive messages, or photos of injuries you have sustained, then this can also help. If your partner checks your phone and your internet history, then this may not be possible and your own (and your children's) welfare must always be your primary concern. Please refer to chapter 5: *Legal Protective Orders* for more information.

Supporting Your Children After Divorce

Children can be greatly affected by their parents' separation and they may need help in dealing with things they have seen or heard, or other issues. Giving them the space to be able to talk to you and to express how they're feeling can be helpful, but sometimes you may feel that they need help beyond what you, as a parent, can provide. In the first place you could talk to their school or your doctor about getting help for them. It's really important that other agencies involved with your children – like their school – are told what has been happening recently. They can then keep an extra close eye on your children and may also be able to point you in the direction of extra help for your children. If social services are assisting your family, then they may also be able to help you to help your children by putting you in touch with other support services.

If you would like to know more about how you can help your children during this difficult time please refer to chapter 14: *Supporting Children through Trauma*. You can also find more information about what to say and do to help children after a separation via Resolution's website *www.resolution.org.uk/information*.

There is also a charity that specialises in helping young people to have a voice and to feel heard when their parents separate. It is currently primarily aimed at 13 to 17 year olds but they intend to extend this so that they cover all children up to the age of 19. *www.voicesinthemiddle.org.uk*

There are also local units designed to help children who are struggling with different issues called Child and Adolescent Mental Health Service (or CAMHS). These services are provided by the NHS and your child can be referred by your GP. For more information visit *youngminds.org.uk*

It can take a long time for children to come to terms with both the separation of their parents, and having witnessed abusive behaviour in their home. It is important to address this by way of accessing help for your children to help them to talk about issues that they may be struggling to understand. It is also important, looking forwards, to help your child understand what a loving and supportive relationship looks like, as their only experience of an adult relationship may have been of an abusive one. This is not something you are able to do alone and it is entirely normal that you would need to access help for your children.

Moving Forward

It can take a long time for you to feel that you are able to put what has happened behind you. You may experience a huge range of emotions including anger, fear, guilt, confusion, powerlessness, loneliness, anxiety and many more. It is perfectly normal and OK to feel anything from absolutely nothing to a whole range of emotions in a short space of time.

You may need professional assistance to come to terms with what has happened to you. You can ask your GP about counselling and other help that may be available to you. They may also be able to provide you with details of local support groups. Having support and people to talk to can be invaluable and this can be found through support groups, through a church or other spiritual group, a hobby group or other parents or friends or family members (or a combination). You can feel isolated when some of your friends or family have not understood the situation you have been in, and you may feel that you need to end some previous relationships to enable you to move forward. Looking at how to find support for you going forward is an important part of healing.

Accessing the right support for you can be a crucial part of helping you to move forward and to deal with the challenges you're facing. Don't be afraid to ask for help and to search out help that you feel will be beneficial to you. Please refer to chapter 15: *Managing Mental and Physical ill Health after Leaving* for further information. The following organisations may also be helpful:

- Women's Aid: www.womensaid.org.uk

- National Domestic Violence Helpline: nationaldomesticviolencehelpline.org.uk Phone: 0800 2000 247

- Refuge: www.refuge.org.uk

The mental health charity MIND also has a section on supporting victims of abuse: *www.mind.org.uk/information-support/ guides-to-support-and-services/abuse/ all-types-of-abuse/#.WyOL2vZFzD4*

TOP TIP Sorting out child residency after leaving an abuser can be a very difficult and challenging time. Be informed, seek professional guidance if need be, take it one step at a time and seek out emotional support from family and friends.

Notes

By Mary Waring

CHAPTER 9

Managing your Money: Budgeting

Coming out of any form of relationship is hugely challenging. Leaving an abuser is even more so, since your confidence may be at an all time low. It is so often easier to stay where you are and where the situation is known, than to break out into uncertainty, even if you know things will be better long term.

Whatever your financial situation when you were with your partner, your finances are likely to suffer because of the separation. You may have very limited funds in your own name and be struggling to get by. Even if you have had a divorce settlement, there will still be less funds than when you and your spouse were living together. You are now in two separate properties with two lots of overheads and

therefore have increased costs when you are living separately, compared with when you were living together. You may have also been subject to financial abuse and been left with debts.

It is therefore vital that you keep track of your spending. If your partner looked after the finances when you were together, it can be very easy to feel overwhelmed at the thought of dealing with them yourself.

But remember, if your partner gave you money each week/month or gave you a specific budget to stick to, you have already been budgeting. So, you may already have all the skills you need. You just haven't perhaps dealt with the responsibility of the whole household budget before.

If you've had the skills to stick to your weekly budget, you have all the skills necessary. If you have not yet left, try to take copies of your last 3 months' bank statements and payslips, or benefits award letters with you. You will need these for opening a new bank account or claiming benefits and they will help with your budget planning.

If you've had the skills to stick to your weekly budget you have all the skills necessary.

How to Budget Accurately

If you haven't previously dealt with the finances, you may be unsure how much your bills come to, or how much money you need per month to get by. This makes it really hard to budget and plan.

So, the first thing to do is keep a **detailed record of all spending**. The more detailed you can be, the better understanding you will have as to where your money is going. Your list should include spending on direct debit, standing order, credit card, debit card, cash etc. Make sure you include items which are paid annually, like car insurance or TV licence.

Cash is often the area where it's easy to lose control of spending. It's so easy to spend a bit here, a bit there, without thinking about it, since each item of spending on its own is very small. But actually, over time, these small items add up to a large figure. So often when our spending seems high we look for the large purchases we've made. But it's not necessarily the large spending items we should be looking at. It's the smaller items that happen on a regular basis, often without us thinking about them, because on their own they seem insignificant.

Whenever you spend, write everything down as you spend it, or preferably in advance of spending it. For example, if you're queuing to buy a coffee, think in advance of what it will cost. So much of our spending happens unconsciously. Becoming aware of what you're spending will be the first step to adjusting the amount you spend.

Sometimes writing it down in advance of actually buying it can act as a brake on spending. Just the fact of writing it down can make you think twice about whether you want to spend that amount or not. You can either **carry a notebook around with you or get a budgeting app** for your phone. Whichever option you choose, make sure you record your spending as soon as that spending happens. If you decide to leave it until the end of the day/ end of the week there's a very high chance you will have forgotten many items.

I suggest you follow this regime for at least three months. If you only do it for a month you will have no way of knowing how representative that month is. It may be that you spent less that month than normal because you were closely monitoring it. Or it may be that it was a particularly expensive month. If you do it for three months you can then start to see a pattern and it will allow you to see what your typical spending is.

Comparing Income and Expenditures

You need to calculate all your income as well, which may include: net pay, child/other benefits, child maintenance or spousal support. If your income exceeds your expenditure, the next step would be to consider how to save and invest this surplus for the future. Please refer to chapter 11: *Financial Planning for the Future*.

However, even if you are in the fortunate position of having more income than you are spending, don't ignore the exercise below regarding *reduction of spending*, since you may find you can increase your surplus income even more.

Although it is suggested you record all your spending for a minimum of 3 months, to do so advisable to continue it throughout the year, so that you can start budgeting for the unusual one off expenses, e.g. car repairs, boiler maintenance, or replacing broken appliances. In addition, there are events that only happen once a year like Christmas, birthdays or summer holiday.

Ensure that you plan in advance so that 1/12th of the annual cost of these things can be set aside each month to cover it. Consider calculating an amount that you would like to save monthly so that you are

not hit with a particularly large bill at any given point, which you are then unable to manage.

Once you have completed this exercise for a year, you will then be fully aware of how much your typical annual spend is. On months when your spending is lower, set aside an extra amount to cover the costs in the more expensive/higher spending months.

If your spending exceeds your income you need to start finding ways to reduce it.

Reduce Spending

Once you have three months' worth of figures from the above exercise, look at it and ask yourself "How can I reduce this figure?". Note, this is a specific question designed to get your brain working towards finding an answer. If you ask yourself "Can I reduce it?", your brain may simply answer "No". Asking a more open question will allow your brain to think more expansively.

Look at every item on your list and see what can be done to reduce the amount you spend. Choose one specific area at a time and see what you can do to get the spending down. When you have that item of spending reduced, look at the next area. This is an exercise to repeat at regular intervals if you think your spending is beginning to get too high.

Be aware that if you use contactless, it may take several days for the item to be debited against your bank account. How-

> **If your spending exceeds your income you need to start work on ways to reduce your spending.**

ever, if you have been following the above advice and writing your spending down, you will know what spending has already hit your bank account and what hasn't.

Using **cash only** for purchases is one way to reduce spending. This has a natural break, in that when your funds have been exhausted that month, you can't spend any further. Research has shown that even if we pay back the balance in full each month, we generally spend twice as much on credit cards as we do if we pay cash.

Shop around - it's surprising how much money you can save. There are of course now so many helpful sites on the internet and below are just a few examples. These are not necessarily the only ones, or even the ones to be recommended. I have simply mentioned a few that spring to mind.

www.uswitch.com will allow you to compare your utility prices.

www.moneysupermarket.com will allow you to compare prices on a large number of different products and services.

www.mysupermarket.co.uk will allow you to compare supermarket prices when shopping online.

If there's a specific area where you're looking to save money, just type, "How do I save money on X?" into your search engine.

Do be aware though that most comparison sites are basically advertising. They charge the company to be registered on the site, which means there may be a cheaper option from a company that isn't included.

Shop around - it's surprising how much money you can save.

However, comparison sites are certainly a good starting place to see how much scope you may have to reduce the price you are currently paying for your services.

By shopping around, if your phone, broadband or TV contract, or even insurance are due for renewal, you can ring your provider saying that you are wanting to leave and give details of a cheaper deal - they may make you an even better offer and save you the paperwork!

But if you've had the skills to stick to your weekly budget you have all the skills necessary.

For further ideas on how to reduce spending please refer to chapter 10: *Dealing with Debt*.

Council tax

Council tax bills assume that two adults occupy the property. If you are living on your own or only with children, there is a 25% reduction- the single person discount.

The following link should help you check whether you are eligible for a discount: *gov.uk/apply-for-council-tax-discount*

Credit

If finances are tight, it will look very attractive to take out a loan or use credit cards, but this should really be a very last resort, and only if you know you can repay the loan or credit card in a short time period.

Most loans are very expensive, and by the time you add interest, the amount you pay back is several times higher than the original loan. It isn't unusual that over the period of the loan you will repay three times the initial amount. So, if you borrow £1,000 you can easily end up paying back £3,000 in total. And this is based on reasonable interest rates. If you don't have a good credit history your rates may be significantly higher.

Credit cards are extremely expensive, particularly if you only repay the minimum payment each month. You will pay interest on the amount outstanding and then the following month you will pay interest on the interest. As a result, the balance will increase significantly. If you have a short term cash flow issue and need to use a credit card, aim to get it repaid as soon as possible.

Opening a Bank Account

The best place to start may be whatever bank where you had any joint accounts, unless you have an unpaid overdraft. Explain the situation that you have left your partner and wish to set up an account in your own name. You can ask to have any previous joint accounts changed to your partner's name only, once you have sorted out how much money you are leaving in it, as you won't be able to access the money once the account is transferred. However, if you are concerned that your address might be revealed to your abuser by mistake, you should open an account in a different bank and you may even want to consider an online bank. Please refer to *Financial Abuse: Will a new code bring about change?*[1] for more suggestions on how to protect yourself from financial abuse and keep your address secure after leaving an abuser.

Credit Rating

Your ability to be offered a mortgage and receive a credit card will depend on your credit rating.

If all bills, bank accounts, mortgage and credit cards were only in your partner's name, this may cause a problem for you since you may not have a credit history. Lenders like to see that you have a record of borrowing money and paying it back.

If your ex-partner doesn't have a good credit history, and overspends, you should get your name taken off any joint accounts as soon as possible. Even if it's his spending that's causing the problem, if your name is on the account, your credit history is also affected and you will be liable for (have to repay) any debts.

If you are still with your partner, this of course may be easier said than done. You may be able to suggest that if your name isn't on the accounts, this will be saving your credit history intact for when, as a couple, you may want to rely on your credit history in the future.

Ask your existing bank to cancel your name from any previous joint credit card and issue one just in your name.

Getting a Credit Card or Loan

Ask your existing bank to remove your name from any previous joint credit card and issue one just in your name. If you haven't previously had a credit card in your name, you may have difficulty getting one, since some lenders rely on your credit history.

Be sure never to use credit cards unless you are able to repay them in full each month. Using your credit card and repaying in full each month will help your credit rating. If you fail to repay in full each month the interest on your purchases can quickly get out of control.

Only ever go to the standard high street banks when looking for a credit card or loan. Be careful of allowing too many banks to do a credit search on you. All financial institutions need to ask you to sign your permission for them to do a search. Doing a search leaves a mark on your credit report to say someone has searched you. The details of the search aren't available.

If you have a number of searches in a short period of time, it looks as though you went to Bank A, who searched you and rejected you, and then you went to Bank B etc. It may be that you went to several banks purely to see what they would lend you and at what rate, but this won't be obvious from looking at your record.

If you speak to a bank, they should be able to give you an estimate of what they would lend you and advise you of the rate before they search you. It's worth having a long phone call rather than just applying online to a number of different banks. A decent bank should be able to say you wouldn't pass their checks, if it's unlikely that you would. It is worth spending the extra time doing this to protect your credit rating.

Car Insurance: No Claims Discount

If your car is insured in your husband's

name & you are just a named driver, you may not be accruing your own no claims discount. For some insurers the no claims is only built up in the main policy holder's name.

It is worth talking to your insurance company to check the situation. If you each have a car, ask the insurance company if it is possible to have a separate policy in your name, under a linked policy. Some insurance companies do allow named drivers to build their own No Claims Discount. So, it will depend on exactly what policy your insurance company offers.

Benefits and Universal Credit

Universal Credit is a payment to help with your living costs. It's paid monthly, and you may be able to get it if you're on a low income, unable to work due to sickness or caring responsibilities, or out of work. Whether you can claim Universal Credit depends on where you live, and on your circumstances.

Universal Credit is being introduced in stages across the UK. If you are making a new claim for benefits, you may have to claim under the old system for a while. If you are already on benefits, you don't need to do anything until you hear from the Department for Work and Pensions (DWP) about moving to Universal Credit, unless you have a change in circumstances.

Universal Credit will replace the following benefits:
• Child Tax Credit

• Housing Benefit
• Income Support
• income-based Jobseeker's Allowance (JSA)
• income-related Employment and Support Allowance (ESA)
• Working Tax Credit

If you currently receive any of these benefits, you can't claim Universal Credit at the same time.

You may be able to get Universal Credit if you're on a low income or out of work.

Eligibility
You may be able to get Universal Credit if you're on a low income or out of work. The Citizens Advice site has a link for you to check eligibility *www.citizensadvice.org.uk/benefits/universal-credit/before-you-apply/Check-if-youre-eligible-for-Universal-Credit/*

The following government site has a link to a benefits calculator to check what benefits you could get if you're not eligible for Universal Credit:
www.gov.uk/benefits-calculators

What you'll get: your Universal Credit payment is made up of a standard allowance plus any extra amounts that apply to you, for example if you:
• have children
• have a disability or health condition
• need help paying your rent

Your circumstances are assessed every month, and what you're paid may change. The rules are very complicated. I would suggest you call the Universal Credit helpline to discuss your situation. Free phone: 0800 328 9344

Support

Dealing with all that is involved when you leave your partner can be overwhelming. At a time when you are at a very low ebb emotionally, then somehow you need to find extra capacity to deal with finances. This can be really tough, particularly if you haven't dealt with the finances before.

My suggestion is to bring someone with you to meetings at the bank and with other finance professionals. If you're feeling overwhelmed, you may not remember all that's been discussed. Your friend can hopefully take notes & ask questions if there are areas you don't understand. Just having someone with you for moral support can be really helpful.

If you don't have someone to come with you, ask if you can record the call on your phone. This at least gives you the opportunity to go back and listen again. If you're unsure about anything after the meeting, send an email or letter rather than making a phone call. Having something in writing gives you the opportunity to keep re-reading it if you're not sure what it means. Also, you can forward it to a friend to see if they can help you understand it.

A final word

Be kind to yourself. This is a very difficult time for you, so acknowledge this and recognise you can't deal with everything in one go. Break all the tasks down into small, manageable chunks and celebrate your achievements when you have completed each one.

It's likely to be a long journey. So just take it one small step at a time.

Some useful sites: UK

- Money Advice Service (Free & impartial money advice): www.moneyadviceservice.org.uk
- Citizens Advice: www.citizensadvice.org.uk/debt-and-money
- Step Change: www.stepchange.org/debt-info/your-financial-situation/making-a-budget
- Savvy woman: www.savvywoman.co.uk
- Christians Against Poverty run free CAP Money budgeting courses: www.capmoney.org

Reference

1 Bate, Marisa. (Oct 2018). Financial abuse: Will a new code bring about change? Retrieved from: www.theguardian.com/money/2018/oct/13/financial-abuse-code-bring-change?fbclid=IwAR1i c11qQM6sx1kZfzICW-uGe-8L-cCrD6ue_1DsB5Dw44LM5Q4KwOMgcn8

 TOP TIP Budgeting might feel overwhelming but if you take it one step at a time your finances will become manageable.

Notes

By Deborah Hewitt

CHAPTER 10

Dealing with Debt

Debt can arise in many ways. Your previous financial situation may have been quite comfortable and you now find you are struggling to manage on much less. You may have been subject to financial abuse, or have been living in a difficult situation because of your ex partner's overspending, addiction to alcohol, gambling etc. You may have had all accounts and bills in joint names and have been left with your ex partner's share of the debts. However you find yourself in this position, no-one is judging you. If you are or think you might be in debt, it's important to remember 3 things:

1) **Do** deal with debt as soon as possible - it will get worse if you leave it.
2) **Don't** panic - for every level of debt, there is a solution.
3) **Do** get help if you need to - mistakes can be expensive. See Resources below.

In complex cases **it is recommended that you seek specialist advice; but** **from reputable, preferably free, debt advisors only.** This chapter is an outline, not a complete 'how to' guide; you should seek help if you are threatened with eviction, court proceedings or bailiffs.

Remember - it is vitally important that you don't agree to pay an individual creditor before you have worked through all the steps. Some will push harder than others - usually the creditors who are not a priority, as they know they will be dealt with only after the most important debts have been dealt with. Stay firm!

Dealing with debt is about you taking back control over an important area of your life. It will not only reduce your stress levels, it will also be a real achievement for you, increasing your confidence and self-esteem. You can do this!

Step 1 - assess the situation - creating a Financial Statement

The people and companies you owe money to are called creditors. If you are struggling to make your debt repayments, the first thing your creditors will want to see is a *Financial Statement*. This is basically a list of all your income and all your spending. This is similar to a personal budget, but the amounts which you can include as reasonable spending are set within guidelines based on what a court would allow. That way, should a creditor threaten to take you to court, there will be little point as a court would not award them more.

So the first step is to create a personal/family budget and turn it into a Financial Statement. A budget just means "the money you need/are planning to spend". After reading through this section, it might sound complicated or scary, but if you take it one step at a time it will become manageable. Do as much as you feel able to in one go, then have a

break. You don't have to get everything done at once.

Whether you are doing it yourself or going to a specialist debt advisor, you need to gather 3 sets of paperwork:
- All the income you receive.
- All your spending - bills, housing costs, food, clothes, travel.
- Everyone you owe money to and how much is owed.

> Dealing with debt is about you taking back control over an important area of your life.

You can create your own budget on paper - there is an example 'Budget sheet' at the end of the chapter to help you get started. However, it is easier to use an online budget planner or even a smartphone app - they do the maths for you and organise your spending into different areas so you can see where your money is going and whether this matches your priorities. There are free versions on many money advice sites, for example:

- *www.citizensadvice.org.uk/debt-and-money/budgeting/budgeting/work-out-your-budget*
- *www.nationaldebtline.org/EW/steps/step2/Pages/Step_2_11.aspx*
- *protected.fscs.org.uk/budgeting/top-online-budget-planner-calculators-and-tools*
- *www.getpennies.com*

Whatever method you choose, the first thing to do is to make a record of everything you have spent in the last 1 to 3 months, in as much detail as possible. This includes spending on direct debit, standing order, credit card, debit card, cash etc. You will find your bank statements very helpful - if you use cards rather than cash it will be a fairly complete record, but don't forget to record what you spend with cash that you have withdrawn - there is no category for "I don't know!" Look at your bank statements over a long period if possible, but for at least one month. Make sure you include items which are paid annually, like car insurance or TV licence. It might take several goes before you have everything written down - don't worry, it will still be there if you take a break.

> **It might take several goes before you have everything written down - don't worry, it will still be there if you take a break.**

You will need to calculate everything on your list for the same timescale - usually one month. Once you have the information on each item of spending, add everything up to get a monthly figure - online tools and apps do this for you, or your phone should have a calculator function. Direct debits and standing orders should be added to your budget sheet too. If they are only paid once a year, divide the amount by 12 to get the monthly figure.

If you don't have any records or statements, or your records aren't complete, you can still make a budget but you will need to record your spending as you go. You can collect receipts/ tickets etc, use a small notebook that will fit in your bag or get a budgeting app for your phone. After a week you can start to make a budget, but keep updating it as you go. (It's a good idea to keep doing this for several weeks if you can, to be sure you have included all your spending - some things only happen occasionally.) Turn

a weekly amount into monthly by multiplying by 4.3 (there are 4 and a bit weeks in a month).

Remember to include all the small amounts you spend, they will add up to significant spending over time. For example, if you buy a low cost TV guide at 65p a week, you are spending £33.93 a year or £1,527 over your lifetime!

Also remember to put aside money to save for big items that will need replacing - cookers & washing machines don't last forever but are fairly essential. Once-a-year expenses like birthday and Christmas presents need saving up for too - planning ahead and spreading the cost means you don't get nasty bills dropping through the door unexpectedly, wrecking your plans.

You will also need to add up your income - all the money you get, including wages, benefits and child support. Now compare your total income with your total spending. If your income is less than you need to repay your debts, or is even less than you are spending, you will need to reduce your spending and if possible to increase your income.

Step 2- Increase Your Income

There are Benefits advice websites like www.gov.uk/benefits-calculators and benefits-calculator.turn2us.org.uk which you can check to make sure you aren't missing any income you are entitled to, or Citizens Advice can do a check for you. The budgeting websites listed above also have a lot of good advice.

Step 3 - Reduce Spending

Creditors will expect you to make every effort to free up income to repay your debts.

Look carefully at each item in your budget. Start by looking at the priorities - what you need rather than what you would like. Once the essentials are in your budget you can look at what money is available for the rest. Priorities are those things which you need to live on or would carry a penalty if you don't pay (see Priority Debts below). Some things are obvious, like paying the rent/mortgage so you don't get evicted, but not paying council tax can lead to a large fine or even prison. Similarly, having a TV without a licence or a car without tax and insurance are heavily penalised.

Look at each item of spending and think about how you can reduce it. Ask yourself 3 questions:

1. Do I need this, or can I cut it out altogether? (Are you actually using that gym membership/reading the magazine you subscribed to?)
2. Can I cut back on the amount I am doing/using this? (Do I need this many takeaways or can I cook it myself? Do I need to buy a coffee on the way to work every day or can I buy a reusable cup and take one from home?)
3. Can I cut the cost of this by buying cheaper? Shop around - it's surprising how much money you can save. If you have a choice don't use the same supermarket every week for non-perishable items (things that don't go off) - each company has different offers and regular prices. For example, you may find you buy your breakfast cereals from one but soap powder from another.

The bad news is that some items will need cutting out of a Financial Statement - this is where it differs from a normal personal budget. Creditors won't accept large amounts of spending on leisure activities and generally refuse to accept allowances for smoking/vaping. There will also be limits on the amount you can spend on clothes, TV or phone contracts, even food and drink, depending on how much you owe and how long it will take to repay. If you are unsure about any of this, look for advice online or make an appointment with a free debt advisor (see Resources).

> Creditors won't accept large amounts of spending on leisure activities and generally refuse to accept allowances for smoking/vaping.

Don't buy more than you need: in 2017, the average UK household threw away £470 worth of still edible food. That's £21,150 over your lifetime! Simple things like planning your meals, then writing a shopping list will help keep costs down - as long as you only buy what's on the list! Special offers can be tempting, but will you use it? There are a lot of money-saving ideas on TV and the internet these days, particularly for food and clothes.

Shop around. Sadly, loyalty is not rewarded. The best deals are usually given to new customers only. But by shopping around you may get a cheaper quote for your insurance, phone, broadband or TV contract when up for renewal. You can then ring your provider saying that you are wanting to leave and give details of the cheaper deal, they may be willing to match it or provide an even better deal.

TV programmes like BBC's 'Eat Well for Less' can be a useful source of advice. They also show how much money can be saved by avoiding brand name products, when supermarkets' own lines are often just as good. Try the "blind taste test" on your children if you think they won't eat something different - they may surprise you.

Use Cash. If you are looking to reduce your spending, try to use cash for purchases. You can see exactly how much money you have left and once it's spent, it can't be spent again - unlike money in the bank. Debit cards don't actually take money out immediately, it can take up to 3 working days for a debit to be processed, so it may look as if you have money left when you don't.

> If you are looking to reduce your spending, try to use cash for purchases.

Work out how much money you will need for a week, then only put that much cash in your purse. If you are working it out from a monthly total, remember to divide the monthly amount by 4.3 (there are 4 and a bit weeks in a calendar month). Don't be tempted to take out any extra, but if you do, take that amount off the money you have left for the rest of the month. If you have some money left at the end of the week, try putting it away in a jar for "rainy day" money - it soon adds up!

The exception to this is paying bills - direct debits or standing orders work out cheaper than cash payments.

Include Your Children. A major source of over-spending for some parents is "pester power" - your children can be very persuasive, and you may feel you want to make it up to them for the family breakdown (even though this is not your fault). Make budgeting and saving money a game that you all play together. If you manage to cut your spending to the point where you have a bit of money left at the end of the month, spend it on a treat for you all. But ask them to make a 'wish list' of treats they really want, so they don't choose something just because it's the first idea they had. Looking forward to treats is called 'delayed gratification' and it's a good skill for parents to teach their children. Budgeting gives the perfect chance to do this!

What if I just made an impulse purchase or signed a contract I can't afford? Although it's not a legal right, many large chain stores will refund money on items you have decided you don't want within 28 days of purchase, provided they are still in their original condition and with a receipt. If you bought goods, or signed up to a service online or by phone, you have an automatic 14 day 'cooling off period' if you change your mind (including finding it cheaper elsewhere) or realise you can't afford it.

If you cannot afford payments on a contract for services, you can stop paying the agreed amount and have the remainder of the money you owe treated as a debt. It will usually mean losing the service you were paying for though. Goods like furniture are more complicated - contact the Citizens Advice consumer helpline on **03454 04 05 06** if you need more advice.

Step 3 - Make a List of your Debt
Once you have your income and spending worked out, but before deciding on a solution, debts need to be divided into 2 types: priority and non-priority.

Priority debts are those things which you need to live on or would carry a penalty if you don't pay. It is important to use your money to settle these debts first. The following are all priority debts:

- mortgage/rent, council tax
- gas, electricity, coal or oil for heating
- child maintenance payments
- Social Fund loans, Benefit and Tax Credit overpayments

- tax debts
- magistrates' court fines, parking penalty charges
- hire purchase or conditional sale of essential goods/furniture
- TV licence

Secondary or non-priority debts are debts where the creditor hasn't got extra powers to make you pay (eg they cannot repossess your home or have you sent to prison). This means these debts can usually be treated differently to priority debts. Common non-priority debts include:

- water rates (domestic customers cannot be cut off - but you should still pay for what you are using, to avoid increasing the debt)
- credit card and charge card debts
- personal loans with finance companies, bank or building society loans and overdrafts
- catalogues and store cards

- personal debts to friends and family
- doorstep-collected loans
- payday loans
- business debts

It is often these non-priority debts which are chased the ha rdest, as the creditor knows they are a lower priority. If you are being pressured t oo hard, you may want to use a third party to negotiate with these creditors (see De bt Solutions). If you are being threatened or intimidated, e.g. by doorstep loan sha rks, you should ring the police immediately. If you borrowed money from someone who isn't FCA authorised, you haven't broken the law, they have.

Step 4 - Debt Solutions

There are differe nt debt solutions availa- ble, depending on whether your debts are priority or seconda ry, how much is owed and how much the repayments need to be, compared with your income or assets (property, saving s or investments). It's also important to consider what you feel you can cope with - it may be a relatively small debt but if you are struggling to cope because of t he abuse or ongoing stressful situations, it may be better to get help (see Resources below). Each type of solution has positives and negatives. See *www.gov.uk/option s-for-paying-off-your- debts for details*.

You can pay your debts in instalments by setting up:

An informal agreement with your creditors

That is, one you make yourself. It means you have some discretion to decide what your priorities are, for example you may want to continue giving to church, or feel you need to repay family members, even though they are seen as a non-priority. If your other spending is within the guide- line amounts and your repayment offer isn't going to take too long, many cred- itors will be reasonable. But an informal agreement means you will have to deal with creditors yourself, and they can put a lot of pressure on you. Also, they don't have to agree to what you propose and may try to threaten you with bailiffs or court proceedings, so you have to be pre- pared to tough it out.

A formal Debt Management Plan (DMP)

This is an agreement with your credi- tors managed by a financial company, or a Debt Payment Programme from the Debt Arrangement Scheme in Scot- land. To find out more go to *www.cit- izensadvice.org.uk/debt-and-money/ debt-solutions/debt-management-plans/ getting-a-debt-management-plan/ choosing-a-debt-management-plan-pro- vider/* or *www.moneyadviceservice.org. uk/en/tools/debt-advice-locator*. This is often less hassle than doing it yourself, but many companies charge fees and this may end up increasing your debts. There are free DMP services available, including those from Christians Against Poverty capuk.org. The company will set your spending amounts for you, which means the DMP has a higher chance of being accepted by creditors, but you have less say about which creditors are paid first, or how much you have to spend on non- priorities.

An Administration Order

When you've had a county court judg- ment (CCJ) or a High Court judgment

(HCJ) against you for debts under £5,000 and you can't pay all at once, you make a monthly payment to your local court and they divide this money between your creditors. It stops creditors on the administration order taking any further action against you without the court's permission.

An Individual Voluntary Arrangement (IVA)

Or Protected Trust Deed in Scotland is an agreement with your creditors to pay all or part of your debts, which is managed by an insolvency practitioner. This is more for people with large debts or who are running their own business. You make regular payments to an insolvency practitioner who will divide this money between your creditors. An IVA can give you more control of your assets than bankruptcy and will stop your creditors taking action against you for your debts. There are fees, so make sure you know how much it's going to cost before hiring an insolvency practitioner. If you do not keep up your repayments, the insolvency practitioner can make you bankrupt, but you may still be able to keep your business running if you have one.

If you **cannot pay your debts** because you do not have enough money for repayments, or assets you can sell, you can apply for a:

Debt Relief Order (DRO)

Which deals with your debts if you owe less than £20,000, do not have enough spare income and do not own your home. Your creditors cannot recover their money

Whichever debt solution you decide on, it will usually mean agreeing not to create any more debt until everything is paid off.

without the court's permission and you're usually freed ('discharged') from your debts after 12 months. You get a DRO from the official receiver, but you must apply through an authorised debt advisor. They'll help you fill in the paperwork. You must follow rules called 'restrictions' e.g. if you want to open a bank account, you have to tell the bank or building society about your DRO.

Bankruptcy Order.

You can apply for yourself, or a creditor can make an application. This should be a final option if all others are not available to you, as your home and other assets may be sold. See www.gov.uk/bankruptcy

It is important for survivors to note that if you get an IVA, DRO or bankruptcy, your name and address will normally be included in a central registry which is **open to public search**. You can apply to have your address removed if publishing it will put you at risk of violence by applying for a **Person At Risk of Violence (PARV) order** - go to *www.gov.uk/bankruptcy/parv-order.*

Whichever debt solution you decide on, it will usually mean agreeing not to create any more debt until everything is paid off. To avoid doubt - this means not using credit of any kind. It's a good idea to think of "credit" as "debt" anyway, as this is what it is!

Doing It Yourself

This chapter is an outline, not a complete 'how to' guide, so if you do decide you

can handle it yourself, take a look through the websites (please see Resource section in the appendix) for more detailed advice. They have budget sheets, details of how to calculate repayment offers and templates for letters you will need to send to creditors. Citizens Advice will also give you help if you ask for an appointment.

Always communicate with creditors **in writing**, so you have a record of what was said. If they phone you or turn up on your doorstep, ask them to write or email, then politely ring off/close the door.

Read letters very carefully. Creditors and collection agencies of non-priority debts use language like "you may be taken to court" or "we may send bailiffs". It's easy to read these sentences without noticing the word "may" - usually these are just tactics to pressure you into agreeing to their demands. Often they are trying to get preferential treatment or get you to agree to pay them before someone else. Take a deep breath, remember "**don't panic**" and file the letters away.

Deal with priority creditors first - and don't ignore letters or deadlines from them. They have legal remedies which they can use. It's important that you request that creditors **stop adding interest or penalties** on to your debt, or you are chasing a moving target. Use the template letters on advice sites.

Bailiffs - what you need to know (England & Wales).
People often think bailiffs are the most scary part of being in debt, but they are governed by strict national standards and can't just help themselves to your prop-

erty without warning. They also have to follow special rules if you have children/ are pregnant, don't speak English well, are disabled or are in a stressful situation such as fleeing domestic abuse.

If they arrive at your door, **don't let them in** - make sure your child or a visitor doesn't open the door. This includes not leaving a door or ground floor window unlocked - they can use these to get in. Speak through the letterbox or small/upstairs window. Ask for proof of who they are and why they're visiting. A 'debt collector' doesn't have the same powers as bailiffs. If they say they're a bailiff or enforcement agent, ask them to show you ID - all registered bailiffs have to carry proof of who they are - and details of the company they work for and the creditor. **Then immediately seek help from a debt advisor.** Call 999 if you feel you're being physically threatened by a bailiff.

If you decide to let them in and you can't afford to pay what you owe straight away you'll normally have to make a 'controlled goods agreement'. This means you'll agree to a repayment plan and pay some bailiff fees. If you break this, they can issue a 'notice of intention to re-enter' and on the next visit they can force entry by using a locksmith. The only other case where they can force entry is if they are collecting unpaid magistrates court fines, or tax debts for HMRC. See *www.gov.uk/ government/publications/bailiffs-and-enforcement-agents-national-standards.*

If **a bailiff says they're evicting you** instead of collecting a debt you'll need to get specialist advice immediately. See Shelter's website *england.shelter.org.uk/ housing_advice/eviction.*

Rebuilding your credit score

Any debts you have been unable to pay (*defaulted on*), formal debt plans or insolvency will negatively affect your credit score. Many things which you wouldn't consider 'credit' will depend on your credit rating. These can include opening current bank accounts, paying fuel and water bills by direct debit, getting a mobile phone contract - as well as the big things like getting a mortgage. The good news is that having any of these things in the future will count towards your credit rating, so you can rebuild a good rating after having had debts. You can find out your 'credit score' through checking companies who offer a permanently free service like Noddle *www.noddle.co.uk.*

. . . .

Resources (in alphabetical order)
- Christians Against Poverty capuk.org
- Citizens Advice www.citizensadvice.org.uk/debt-and-money
- Debt Advice Foundation www.debtadvicefoundation.org or phone 0800 043 40 50
- Money Advice Service www.moneyadviceservice.org.uk
- National Debtline www.nationaldebtline.org/ or free phone 0808 808 4000
- Stepchange charity www.stepchange.org
- UK Government site www.gov.uk/options-for-paying-off-your-debts

Example Budget sheet

Make sure the amounts are all for the same time period: weekly or monthly.

The first column plus your travel to work/school are likely to be accepted by creditors if the amounts are "reasonable". The rest of the second column will be negotiable and may not be accepted.

Expenditure*:	Amount £:
Rent/Mortgage/Endowment policy	
Secured Loans	
Ground rent/service charge	
Buildings/Contents Insurance	
Council Tax	
Water	
Electricity	
Gas/Oil/Solid fuel	
Mobile phone	
Food & Household cleaning	
Specialist dietary needs	
Toiletries/Make-up	
Clothing/Shoes	
School uniform	
Prescriptions/Dentist	
Optician/Eyewear	
Court/parking fines	
Child Support payment	
Childcare	
School expenses	
TV Licence	
Pension Contributions	
Bus/Train/Taxi fares	
Car Purchase	

Expenditure*:	Amount £:
Bus/Train/Taxi fares	
Car Purchase	
Car Insurance	
Vehicle Tax	
MOT/Maintenance	
Petrol/Diesel	
Future needs: Car Repairs	
Breakdown membership	
Landline/Internet	
Digital Rental (TV/Streaming)	
Appliance Rental/Hire Purchase	
Credit/Store card Repayments	
Other unsecured loan repayments	
Life Insurance	
Pet Food/Insurance/Vet bills	
Leisure Activities	
Gym/Club membership: you	
Gym/Club membership: Children	
Religious/Charity Giving	
Future needs: Birthdays/Christmas/holidays	
Future needs: replacing appliances	
Future needs: house repairs/decorating	

*This list isn't exclusive - add your own unique expenditures as well.

Notes

By Mary Waring

CHAPTER 11

Financial Planning for your Future

You should always aim to have rainy day money in a bank account. This is to ensure that if your income stream stops, (for example due to ill health and you being unable to work) you have sufficient emergency funds to cover your needs.

In an ideal world, you should have three months' worth of your spending in a bank account. If you haven't been able to save before now, this is going to take a while to achieve, but set this as your aim to work towards. Only once you have three months' worth of your spending in a bank account should you consider any other investments.

This chapter will explain the basics of how a bank savings account, an Individual Savings Account (ISA) and pension plan work and will hopefully encourage you to start saving into at least one of these options. Both the ISA and pension plan have specific tax advantages. Which one is most appropriate for you depends on your priorities and circumstances.

Use this chapter to provide the background you need, but then do talk to an advisor to determine which investment strategy is right for you.

Bank Savings Account

The easiest way to save is to put money into a bank account. However, you will have seen that the interest rate payable on a cash deposit is very low. In the UK currently, the rate may be as low as 0.1%. You will get a higher interest rate if you are willing to keep your money tied up for a longer period, but it will still be a reasonably low rate. Rates for a 1 year deposit are generally between 1% and 1.5%.

The reason for this low rate of interest is the relationship between risk and reward when investing. The greater the risk you are willing to take, the greater the return (reward) you'll get. Money in a bank account is generally considered to be risk-free. In the UK, unless a bank becomes bankrupt, (and even then, you are covered up to £85,000 if the bank is covered under the Financial Services Compensation Scheme) your money in the bank is safe. As a result, the return you get is low.

> The easiest way to save is to put money into a bank account. However, you will have seen that the interest rate payable on a cash deposit is very low.

Individual Savings Account (ISA)

To get us all saving as much as possible, the UK government allows tax advantages when saving into an ISA. Annual limits are set as to how much you can save into an ISA each year and receive the tax benefits. The current limit in the UK for tax year 2018/19 is £20,000, and can be invested either in cash, stocks and shares, or a mixture of each.

The tax benefits relating to ISAs are explained in detail below.

Ordinarily, if you invest in the stock market and your investment increases in value (which of course you hope it will), you would suffer capital gains tax on the increase. For example, if you invested £40,000 into a stocks and shares portfolio, and that grew over time to £70,000, you would have made a capital gain of £30,000.

Under the current rules, £11,700 of this gain is not subject to a tax charge. The balance of £18,300 will be taxed at 18% or 28% dependent on whether you are a basic rate or higher rate taxpayer. Therefore, the tax charge will be between £3,294 and £5,124.

However, if the £40,000 had been invested over several years in various ISAs, the £30,000 gain would be totally tax free. As a result, you would have additional cash of between £3,294 and £5,124 depending on your tax position.

Additionally, if you had invested outside an ISA plan, you would need to pay income tax on any interest or dividends received from your investments. However, with an ISA, no tax needs to be paid; neither income tax nor capital gains tax. The one exception is that the 10% tax paid on a dividend cannot be reclaimed.

If you have the means to put savings away each year into an ISA, over time this can add up to a significant sum for your future. You can draw against your funds at any time and draw whatever amount you wish. If you needed to, you could withdraw your full amount in one transaction, without any consequences.

Private Pension Plans

Using a pension to save for your future also has very attractive tax advantages.

Let's assume you want to invest £100 per month into your pension plan. If you're a basic rate taxpayer, paying tax at 20%, you actually pay in £80 per month from your bank account. The pension provider will then reclaim £20 from the tax office (HMRC). When added to the £80 you invested from your bank account, this makes up your £100 contribution. Basically the tax office gives you back the tax you've paid.

If you're not earning but have some funds to invest, you can invest a maximum of £2,880 each year and the government will immediately top it up to £3,600, giving you an additional £720. These tax advantages aren't well known, so do consider pensions if you are looking to invest long term.

When can you draw your pension?

Under the current rules, you can access your private pension once you are aged 55. This age is increasing since it is expected to always be 10 years below the state pension age. Be cautious of anybody who tells you they can help you to access your cash before the age of 55 – unless you have an illness or belong to a certain type of scheme this is usually pensions liberation and is often fraud.

Under the new rules from 2015, your pension is very flexible, and can almost be viewed as a bank account, to draw amounts as and when you need them. You may want to draw large amounts in one year and then very little in the following.

25% of the amount drawn is tax free and the balance you draw is chargeable to income tax in the year you withdraw it. You can, if you wish, withdraw the whole amount of your fund in one amount. However, this may result in a ridiculously large tax bill and therefore is unlikely to be the best route.

An alternative option is to get an annuity, whereby you swap your lump sum for a stated monthly income that is payable for the rest of your life. This is less flexible in the sense that you have no option to draw extra in any year. However, it has the advantage that it guarantees to pay you a certain amount per year for as long as you live.

As a very rough approximation, a lump sum of £100,000 for a healthy, non-smoker aged 65, would provide an annual income of circa £4,500. Whilst this doesn't sound a lot, remember a healthy 65 year old may live for 25-30 years. The income on an annuity is payable for life. Therefore, the longer you live the greater value you are getting.

Of course, it does mean that the shorter the period of time you live, the lower the value of the annuity for you. You don't know in advance how long you will live, so

Using a pension to save for your future also has very attractive tax advantages.

the decision will often be made based on how concerned you are that your money will run out if it is invested.

State Pension

The current full UK state pension is £164.35 per week, so £8,546 per annum, payable from state pension age. State pension is currently index-linked, which means it will increase by inflation each year. This means it will continue to be worth an equivalent amount in relation to the cost of living.

To find your state pension age, visit gov.uk/state-pension-age. Remember, state pension age is increasing so do review this at regular intervals.

In order to receive a full state pension, you need to have paid or been credited with 35 years' worth of National Insurance Contributions. For each year less than 35 that you have achieved, you will get 1/35th less money each week.

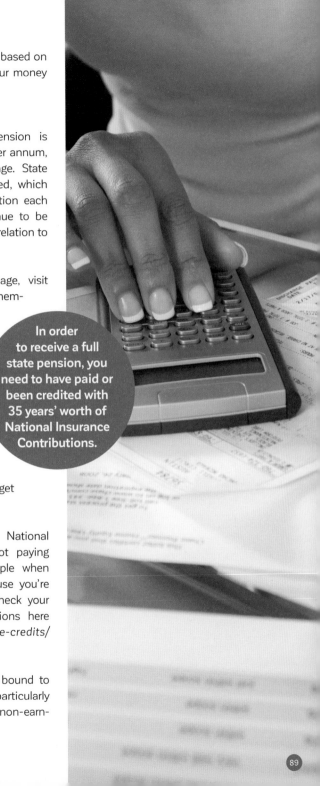

In order to receive a full state pension, you need to have paid or been credited with 35 years' worth of National Insurance Contributions.

You may be able to get National Insurance credits if you're not paying National Insurance, for example when you're claiming benefits because you're ill or unemployed. You can check your eligibility to receive contributions here www.gov.uk/national-insurance-credits/eligibility

Do not assume that you are bound to receive a full state pension, particularly if you have spent time as a non-earning spouse or partner. If you haven't yet achieved your full 35 years, you can normally make voluntary contributions, to increase your state pension entitlement.

My recommendation is for you to obtain a statement so that you can see what amount of contributions you can make, and what the impact will be on your additional income. Details as to how to do this are available at *www.gov.uk/check-state-pension*

It is likely that it will be well worth paying additional contributions so you can increase your state pension. I suggest you obtain a statement and find out what amount you can pay, or whether you should be paying voluntary contributions going forwards.

> It is likely that it will be well worth paying additional contributions so you can increase your state pension.

Stock Market

What about investing in the stock market? Over time, investing in the stock market will provide greater return than investing in a bank account. This is due to the greater risk you are taking.

If you invested £100 in a bank account, the value of your deposit would never fall below £100. However, when you invest in the stock market, the stock market goes down as well as up, so there is every likelihood that at times your investment is worth less than £100.

However, provided you don't need to access your investment at that stage and can leave it there, over time history shows us the stock market has always

recovered and has produced a significantly higher return than funds in a deposit account.

For this reason, I only recommend money is invested in the stock market if you are willing to leave it there for a minimum of three years, and possibly five to be on the safe side.

If you need to access your funds within the short term (less than three years) and you have invested in the stock market, there is a high risk that your money may have dropped in value during that time. That is why stock market investing is for those with a longer term time horizon. If you can take a much longer term view, you can choose not to access your funds when the market has dropped.

If you can leave your money there long term, falls in the value will still be difficult to deal with. But provided you don't need to withdraw your funds at that stage and can leave them there to recover, your long term financial wealth shouldn't be affected. If the thought of losing money would give you sleepless nights, maybe you should consider how suited you are to invest in the stock market.

If you do decide to take this route, the two options you should initially consider are ISA and pension, which I have discussed in the previous section, due to the very attractive tax advantages available with each of them.

Summary

Some areas of this chapter have been reasonably technical to be able to cover the tax issues involved.

Investing for the future, especially when you invest in the stock market, is not straightforward. As soon as you expose your money to the chance of an increase due to the investment returns, you are also exposing it to the chance of a fall in value.

Having a well diversified portfolio in a large number of funds is essential, to protect you as much as possible against volatility in the stock markets.

Where possible, if you can afford to, please do take financial advice from a professional before investing.

Make sure you do significant research before committing to any investment. One important thing to remember is the maxim "If it looks too good to be true, it probably is". There are a lot of fraudsters around. Be wary of anyone who offers very high returns and particularly if you're told the returns are guaranteed.

Investing in the stock market involves risk. But a well-diversified, well-run portfolio will provide greater returns over the long term than keeping your funds in a bank account.

Notes

TOP TIP Only once you have three months' worth of spending in a bank account, to cover your needs, should you start to consider any other financial plans.

By Robin McKay Bell

CHAPTER 12

Career Planning

And what do you do? is a question commonly asked in many social situations. Without an easy answer most people will feel small and inadequate because identity is so often connected to work. Yet there may be logical reasons for unemployment: a partner who wouldn't allow you to work; responsibilities with children; caring for an elderly parent; perhaps a lack of confidence in returning to work after a break.

It's important to remember that lots of women have successfully returned to work, even after many years away from paid employment. These chapters, _Career Planning_ and _Returning to Work_, are intended to _motivate_ and _empower_ you. I include suggestions for getting short-term jobs as well as working towards long-term goals. Defining your ideal job, which may be a long-term goal, is a good way to start your career plan. Then, by working backwards from that goal, you

may see a path that leads you there, with steps along the way.

A lack of confidence is usually the first major obstacle in returning to work after an extended absence. You may have questions such as: _Do I still have skills that make me employable? How do I even begin a job search? Who will hire me after I've been unemployed for so long? What will I put on my CV to cover the gaps in employment?_

It takes a bit of work to find answers that will help you grow your confidence, but with a bit of time and effort you can make a career plan for yourself. In the following chapter, I will show you some tools and techniques to move forward with job search, applications and interviews.

However, if your need to get a job is urgent, you can jump forward to a section in the next chapter called *"The Quick Fix"* for short-term job strategies. You can always return to this chapter later, once you have solved your immediate problem.

The first step in planning your career is self-knowledge. Do this work at your own pace, in a quiet moment when you have time for reflection. I suggest using a notebook so you'll have a record of your responses.

When you're doubtful about yourself it helps to remember times of happiness and success.

Eight Personal Signposts

When you're on a road, signposts help you find where you're going. In this section, they point the way towards a career. Some signposts are answers to questions, others are lengthy exercises designed to establish what your skills and experience are, and where you may fit in the job market. The first three signposts are an aid to regaining your self-confidence.

Signpost No.1: Joy

When you're doubtful about yourself it helps to remember times of happiness and success.

Think of a time you were happy at work and in a paid role. The first thing that comes to mind is likely to be important. Where were you? What were you doing? Write it down.

Everyone has had moments of joy at work. If nothing occurs to you, return to this question later – or wait for the answer to arrive when you least expect it.

Signpost No.2: Self-employment

Other than regular jobs, what have you been paid to do? Write down any jobs you've had where you've been paid directly, possibly with cash. Avoid listing those that involved drudgery. The best ones are those that made you happy at the time. You might have done them at any point in your life from childhood to the present. (Some examples might be: gardening, copy editing or writing, cooking or baking, running a stand at a local fair, bookkeeping for a friend or family member.)

After you've done that consider this question: *Would anyone pay you to do one of those jobs now?* Sometimes the answer to an immediate need is close at hand.

Now that you've recalled some positive feelings about work, your answer to the next question will point the way towards your *motivated skills*, those that are so natural to you that you are always at your best when using them.

Signpost No.3: Your speciality

What do people come to you for? There is something that you do – or once did – that makes you special. Are you good at explaining things? Are you the one who gives sound advice to friends or children? Do you enjoy planning outings or journeys? Do people come to you for your great recipes? Or financial advice?

Those are a few examples. You may have more than one speciality. Write down any that come to mind. If you're stuck, ask a trusted friend or relative – they'll probably have a ready answer for you.

This is a powerful signpost. If you can find a job that allows you to use one of your motivated skills you're very likely to succeed in it.

Signpost No.4: Your skills

A *skill set* is the combination of knowledge, skills and abilities that will connect to a particular job. It's important for you to be able to identify your skill set in order to make a career plan. Start by making a list of what you consider to be your top five skills, e.g. problem-solving, organisation, communication, Microsoft Office skills, online skills (your list will, of course, be different).

Once you've completed the list, it's time to move on to an in-depth analysis of your skill set. You're about to do a skills extraction exercise. This is used to discover your *transferable skills*, those underlying competencies you bring to any role or task. They're often so intuitive they are difficult to describe – and there is crossover between your professional and personal life. Transferable skills enable you to make a career change to another role or employment sector and, if you're planning to return to a job you've done

previously, understanding your transferable skills will help you make a better case for yourself.

This exercise takes time and thought to complete properly. Most people find it hard to do in an afternoon or an evening. I recommend you complete the task as an essential part of your career planning.

Exercise

Take a blank sheet of paper, A3 size if you have one. You are going to create a 'mind-map' of you, your employers, jobs and skills. To do this, write your name in the centre of the page, then surround it with the employers you have had. For each employer, list the job titles you held. Make sure you include any voluntary or unpaid roles, e.g. secretary of the local football club. Also include key roles you have held in society, mother included (listing *all* of your roles). The job titles form the second layer of the map. The next layer will be the skills you used in each role.

Here's an example:

Deriving your skills

For each of the jobs on your mind-map spend a few minutes living in the role.

- What did a typical day involve?
- As you think about what you did, keep asking yourself how you did it, why you did it, and what the outcome was.
- What skills did you need for the task?
- What skills did the role develop?
- If someone were to do your role, what would you say were the key skill requirements to succeed?

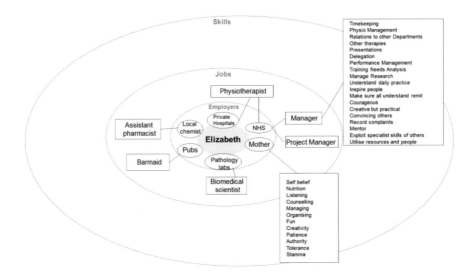

Keep going until you have described, using lots of 'skills' words, what you did in each of the roles. Some examples of skills words are:

analysed	marketed
assisted	motivated
automated	multi-tasked
calculated	organised
communicated	persuaded
created	planned
deduced	prepared
developed	presented
dissected	reviewed
educated	served
entered	sold
handled	supported
innovated	sympathised
inspired	taught
laid out	trained
led	treated
listened	verified
managed	

Repeat the exercise for each of the roles you have held, including volunteer and part-time positions. When you have finished, look at all the skills and job details you have written down and make a list of the words or phrases that are repeated most often which describe the groups of skills you always use in each role. Summarize these as five to ten core skills that you can take to any role, either as a list or as a new mind-map. These are your 'transferable skills'. Whatever job you do, you always bring these to the table.

Signpost No.5: Values

"I never felt I fitted in there", is a statement we've all heard. People often reflect on a previous job and conclude that there was some fundamental mismatch between what they expected from the job and what it actually delivered – maybe it was to do with the way their colleagues behaved, how their boss treated them or with what customers demanded. With hindsight this may have been caused by a clash of values – the principles and standards that each of us hold dear. Fairness, honesty, money as the measure of success, a good balance between work and home life, importance of family; these are all examples of personal values. If there's a big difference between what's important to you and what the company you work for expects, then trouble will ensue.

In planning a career, an honest appreciation of your values plays a key part in ensuring that the work you do will be fulfilling and long-lasting. The need to earn an income may be the overriding motivator to take any role that is offered, but if there is a values mismatch with the company or its employees, that employment will not last long and it will not be fulfilling. Career decisions linked to your values are much more powerful than those linked to your needs.

As a survivor of abuse, you will also need to be aware of the power and control structures within an organisation. They reveal what a company values. You will not want to work for an overbearing boss in an organisation that demands unpaid overtime.

> As a survivor of abuse, you will also need to be aware of the power and control structures within an organisation.

To determine some of your values, the next exercise is relatively easy and a very pleasant task.

Who do you admire? List the names of three people you respect and admire. They may be living or dead. After you've done that, write down why you admire them, then consider what they have in common. Those commonalities are values you own. They are very important to you. Try to find a workplace where they are practised.

Signpost No.6: Interests

You may also be guided by interests; they are often aligned with your values. For example: Are you concerned with animal welfare? How do you feel about environmental issues? Is there a cause that a favourite charity supports? Take a step further and write down three things you are interested in and about which you have strong feelings. They are additional signposts that may point you in the right direction.

Signpost No.7: Opportunities

It's no good defining an ideal job and then discovering there are no opportunities available in your chosen field, or in the area where you live. For example: banks are closing local branches and shedding employees by the thousands. Unless you're a highly skilled financial analyst you're unlikely to find a job in the banking sector. But if you have financial skills, consider that many people are becoming self-employed and are therefore in need of assistance: bookkeeping, accountancy and tax advice are in demand by a growing number of individuals and small companies.

Opportunities exist wherever there is growth or change. The care sector is growing; so is the online sector. We're seeing more boutique cafes and restaurants as more pubs are closing. There are fewer public sector jobs with more roles found in the private sector with companies under contract to local and national governments.

With your list of skills and values to hand, combined with your previous experience, you're now able to research sectors and companies that have growth potential. And research is essential, as you will see in the next chapter.

Signpost No.8: Your financial needs

If you haven't already made a budget, now is a good time to make one - please refer to chapter 9: *Managing Your Money: Budgeting*. In order to determine what salary you will need, you have to know your expenses. As part of planning, it's also good to consider your future needs. Perhaps you're receiving benefits and you'd like to be free of them. How much would you need to earn to achieve that goal? Give this some serious thought, as you'll also need to be realistic about what certain roles will pay.

Once you've recognised and understood your personal signposts, and you've defined your ideal job, it's time to seek a role that may lead to your goal.

Your Ideal Job

Having come this far, you are able to complete a chart that will show you the kind of job you should be seeking. The text in the boxes is there to illustrate how you might start this task. Try to be as specific as you can in each case i.e. "30 minutes maximum travel time", not just "Close to home".

Strategy

Once you've recognised and understood your personal signposts, and you've defined your ideal job, it's time to seek a role that may lead to your goal. For example: working as an admin in a school would logically be a good start if you want to be a teacher. You could then earn a teaching certificate by studying part-time while you are working. Similarly, if your ideal job is in finance where you would use your aptitude for numbers, a part-time role as a bookkeeper would allow you to study for qualifications as an accountant.

As a strategy for employment in the digital jobs market, you might consider a course

MY IDEAL JOB

Essential	Nice to have	Certainly don't want
Part time, school hours	*Close to home; 30 mins*	*Long commute*

in coding software. It's like learning a new language and, contrary to what you might think, you don't need advanced maths skills to learn how to code. Many courses are offered online so you can obtain accreditation without attending a college. (Try the Open University.) There are plenty of app developers that hire coders on a freelance basis. If you have an aptitude for this you might develop a whole new career.

You may want to return to a managerial or professional role that you once held. In that case you will need to reactivate a network in order to learn more about how things are done now and to make new connections that can help you.

Since there are so many sectors and roles I can't be prescriptive about your personal strategy. You will follow your own path, but with the knowledge of your skills and values, combined with an ideal job in mind, you're equipped to move forward to the next chapter for techniques to help you find your next job and reach your destination.

 TOP TIP Assess your values, interests and transferable skills when career planning.

Notes

By Robin McKay Bell

CHAPTER 13

Returning to Work

This chapter provides some practical methods to return to work after a period of absence, based on real-life experiences of women who have successfully regained employment. Having decided on your field of interest, the information below will guide you towards success but it will take some time. If you need a job immediately due to financial concerns, please go to the end of this chapter for some options to consider.

Confidence

Increasing your confidence starts with language and how you speak and think about yourself. Saying "I was made redundant" or "I've just been a stay-at-home mum" will likely make you feel small and inferior – and those statements are not true. No person is redundant; no woman is "just a mum". Instead, say "My *role* was made redundant. I'm looking for new opportunities", or "I'm returning to work and looking for a role in..."

Also start by thinking, "I am the solution to someone's problem." You are not a problem, you are a solution. Once you find your job you'll know that it is true. Whatever the reason you are not working now, you will have learned from the exercises in the previous chapter that you have many skills to offer an employer.

Empowerment

Here are three ways to empower yourself and improve your chances of working again:

1 Volunteering.

Increasingly, employers are beginning to recognise that volunteering is work. It is unpaid work but it is work nonetheless – and it can be included on your CV to cover a gap in employment. Volunteering helps you to reactivate skills, reduce social isolation, improve self-esteem and strengthen your network (or develop a new one).

To find a local volunteering activity, google *volunteer opportunities in [name your local authority]*. If your children are of school age, you might enquire at their schools. You could also try *www.do-it.org* to find volunteer roles within larger, national charities.

2 Job clubs or employability courses.

Job search can be a lonely business. Staring at a computer screen for hours on end, sending applications and getting rejected is de-motivating and harmful to self-esteem. Attending a job club or employability course means you will be with others in a similar situation, gain peer-to-peer support, reduce loneliness, learn contemporary job search skills and find local job opportunities. You will also grow your network. Use Google to search for job clubs or employability courses.

3 Take a course.

Learning a new skill or refreshing an old one is an act of empowerment. The current buzzword is *upskilling*. As well as improving your self-esteem, it's good to include skills upgrades in your CV, especially if you've been away from work for some time. As an example, computer skills are essential for everyone these days. Local adult further education colleges often provide free or subsidised courses. Benefit agencies may also give you support if you enquire.

Job Search

It's been said that 80% of potential job opportunities are 'hidden jobs'– that is, jobs that need to be filled but are not yet public knowledge. However, the majority of job seekers will only apply for a job once it's advertised. If you concentrate your search on advertised jobs you are up against all other applicants. Your odds are much better if you look for a hidden job. When you approach small companies you might be the only applicant.

Note that with public sector roles, hiring follows a formal and standardised process as a legal requirement. However, it is still of benefit to learn about the role before it is open to applications. If possible, try to be referred by someone in the organisation. You will still need to apply formally but your application may find favour if someone has already endorsed you.

I suggest spending around 80% of your time researching organisations, and networking (which is discussed separately below). But do continue to apply to advertised jobs; it is an important part of your job search strategy.

Finding hidden jobs

There are two ways to access the hidden jobs market:

> Volunteering helps you reactivate skills, reduce social isolation, improve self-esteem and strengthen your network

1 Speculative Approach:

Do some research online and find an organisation where you would like to work. Then you can write a letter addressed to a person such as a line manager (*not necessarily* the HR department where it possibly won't be moved forward). Make sure the letter is written well and in a business format. You don't need to include your full postal address, if revealing it makes you nervous - the first part of your postcode will do. Don't include your CV. You're simply making an initial contact and hoping for a response.

Explain what you're looking for, why you think you're suitable and why you want to work for the company (or school or charity – this won't work for a public sector role). Close the letter by inviting an email response or a phone conversation. Be sure to include your email address so the person can contact you.

When you use this method you're playing a long game, but if you're organised and good at record-keeping – so you know what you've sent and when – it can pay off.

2 Networking

Networking is the art of building alliances. You are networking when you develop relationships that help you realise your goals. Social networking is investing time with people you like. Business networking is making contact with people who can introduce you to useful contacts. In a job-seeking context, networking simply means maximising the chance

> **Networking is the art of building alliances. You are networking when you develop relationships that help you realise your goals.**

that someone with a vacancy will learn that you are available. Networking is NOT cold-calling people to ask for assistance or asking friends for a job.

People are your best resource when you're looking for work. If you start from the position that you can help others, you'll network better. For example: if someone assists you, try to return the favour in some way. Because you intend to help them as well, you'll feel genuine when you ask someone for advice or assistance.

Since 70% of jobs are found through networking this is an essential skill to develop. The first thing to do is tell your friends and family what kind of job you're seeking. This is reaching out to your 'first degree' connections: people you know. Be sure *never* to ask for a job directly – it creates an awkward situation. What you want is information and direction towards other people who can assist you: your 'second degree' connections, those people who know your first degree contacts.

If you've had to move locations, you may need to start a new network. However, you will probably have previous contacts you can reach by email or online if you're using social media channels. But only reach out to previous contacts if it won't put you at further risk - the priority is your safety.

What's your story?

When you meet new people it's important to have a rehearsed 'pitch', or as

it's sometimes called, a 'Tell Me About Yourself' or **TMAY**. This is a short but engaging spoken introduction about you and what you have to offer. A good TMAY creates an interest or need in the other person, is between 30 seconds and two minutes in length and ends with (if appropriate) a clear statement about what you are seeking. You'll be asked, 'What do you do?' hundreds of times, so it's best to have a solid response. Of course it will be tailored to who is asking the question and to the context, but the principal points should remain simple and succinct. A TMAY is not an opportunity to give your life story. What people are really asking is: 'Tell me why I should talk to you now or see you again?' Keep it short; all you need is two or three sentences about what you can offer now with some evidence as to your skills and strengths.

Finding advertised jobs

As part of your search, in the UK, you should use job boards/websites. Here are a few of the most popular at the time of writing: www.totaljobs.com, www.monster.co.uk, www.reed.co.uk, www.cv-library.co.uk, www.timewisejobs.co.uk

These are sites where posted jobs are brokered by recruitment agencies – companies in the middle between the employer and you. Therefore recruiters don't like it if you discover the name of the employer and go direct; they are in business to take a fee or percentage of your salary if you're hired. Try to ring the recruiter and establish a relationship but don't expect it to happen. Recruiters don't care about you and will only contact you or connect with you if you're an ideal candidate. You'll need a thick skin when you do this. Remember that no rejection is personal.

When you see a job you like, tailor your CV for the role (see the CV section below.) Then upload it to the job board. Your application will be scanned by a computer programme and passed to the recruiter if it sees enough *key words* to move it forward. As a tip, if you haven't heard back in a week or so, upload the same CV with a different file name: e.g. *Joan Doe CV v2*. The computer will see it as new – recent ones take priority – and put it on top of the pile again. Create and upload a new CV for every application you make. A generic, one-size-fits-all CV will not work, even though some sites invite you to upload one.

Social media for job search

For reasons of safety you may be reluctant to continue with a social media presence. Harassment is the last thing you need when searching for work. However, you should consider that employers look for you online after you've made an application, as do recruiters. Those with a good online presence have a distinct advantage over those who don't. How to handle this dilemma? Use LinkedIn. You can set up a profile page – or modify your current one – and only include your first name in the title, as in Linda M. If your ex is on Linke-dIn he will have to be connected with you to send any messages, unless he has a premium account where he may send a message. In that case you can block him immediately. You may do the same if he uses a friend or proxy to contact you. When you set up your account you can conceal your location. Use caution, however, if your abuser is actively trying to find you, as all social media activity presents a certain level of risk. You may need to weigh up the benefits against the risks of any social media presence, and may feel that you need to err on the side of caution.

LinkedIn is a combination profile page (for employers to view), a networking site (connect with others) and a job search engine where you can find jobs and be found by recruiters who will see your profile; (they pay for the privilege). Use Google to learn how to set up your profile page and especially your safety settings. Understand that it's not an online CV, it's more friendly and personal in tone. Write your Summary Statement in the first person, using "I", and tell a brief story about your skills and what you're seeking. If you do decide to use LinkedIn, you will need a good photo – a head and shoulders shot – to appear credible. That may give you pause but please accept that without it your profile will appear unprofessional. If you don't have one, have a friend take the picture for you on a decent camera phone.

Don't underestimate Twitter. Very often, jobs are posted on Twitter before they appear anywhere else. With your laptop you can view company tweets without having a Twitter account. If you do set one up, follow companies of interest and use hashtags # to see job opportunities, as in #teachingjobs or #adminroles. Install the app on your smartphone and

> Those with a good online presence have a distinct advantage over those who don't. How to handle this dilemma?

use a handle that isn't your name, like @thesmartone instead of @JaneDoe.

Applications

So you've found an opportunity with a job description and it's time to apply. Here's what you need to get started:

1 A desktop or laptop with Internet access, or reliable access to one (libraries will have computers for public use).

2 A 'professional' email address, for example: name.surname@gmail.com. The name should connect with the name on your CV and should not sound flippant. For example: name@icloud.com or name56@tesco.com are acceptable, but chelseano1@anyoldisp.com, dancinglady@myhotmail.com are definitely out. I suggest setting up a gmail account and use it only for job search.

3 A mobile number that will be answered appropriately. It's acceptable in business culture to use your mobile number on applications, instead of your home telephone number. If you do give your home number, inform anyone who is likely to answer the phone that you might receive a call regarding a new job. If using your mobile, then make sure the voice-mail message is appropriate for someone seeking employment.

4 A CV, biography, career summary, resumé, employment history –

whatever the name, you will need a document that accurately reflects who you are and what you are offering for the position. Later in the chapter we will cover the principles of preparing an appropriate CV.

5 A system for recording what you have sent and when, including: the job advertisement, and where you saw it; a copy of the CV that you sent; a record of any previous conversations about the role.

The first step in the application process is to decide whether there is a good fit between you and the role. There are two questions to ask yourself:

1. How many of the *essential* and *desirable* skills and experience criteria do I meet? They're found in the job description. Women will often not apply unless they know they have at least 90% of what is described. Men, on the other hand, will sometimes apply with 60% and succeed. Why? In this regard, men will sometimes bluff and most women won't, it's uncomfortable for most. But consider that while you should have all, or nearly all, of the essentials, it's not necessary to have all of the desirables — they describe a perfect candidate who may not exist. Use your discretion (don't bluff) but also try to exercise some courage.

2. What do I know about the working style of this organisation and how likely am I to fit in? Answering this question involves research.

> The first step in the application process is to decide whether there is a good fit between you and the role.

Online application forms

These are used for all public sector applications and also for larger charities. They're a pain to complete but you must do so if you want the job. You should take your time and be careful with your responses. As a tip, answer the questions on a separate Word document and print it on paper. That way you'll see errors that weren't obvious onscreen and you can spell - and grammar - check before copying and pasting into the relevant box. For longer pieces of text – e.g. your personal statement – have a friend read it.

DON'T send a CV unless asked. Sending one without a request for it signals that you are a person who doesn't follow directions.

When writing your personal statement, consider that it's a brief summary of your education/courses leading to a job, followed by another job, especially including achievements, all the while moving on for reasons of personal growth. Include your top skills and any commendations you may have received. Make a statement about your values that matches the values of the organisation. You will need to tell them why you think you fit in their organisation.

DON'T send a CV unless asked. Sending one without a request for it signals that you are a person who doesn't follow directions – it's a reason to be excluded.

Cover letters and CVs

Here's how it works: cover letters are written so that your CV will be read and considered. The purpose of a CV is to get you an interview. It's a marketing document, not the story of your life. There are countless specialist books that provide guidance on creating a CV and cover letter. We'll cover the basics here.

The key steps are:

1 Reread the advertisement (and/or job description) until you are crystal clear about what the employer seeks. Note any instructions as to how to apply.

2 Compose a covering email or letter and a CV, all of which should be tailored to the role. Describe yourself positively and match your skills to the requirements.

3 Submit your application in the required format by the closing date.

It's not as simple as it sounds. Many companies, and all recruitment agencies, use **ATS** (**A**pplicant **T**racking **S**ystems) to screen CVs. These are software programs that search for *keywords*. If they aren't there, the CV will not be read by a human. So it's a word game: use enough keywords to get past the computer but not so many that it frustrates a person reading the CV if it goes forward. For example: *motivated*, *creative* and *dynamic* are clichés, so overused they have no meaning. But if you see them in the job description you must include them at least once in the first half of the top page in order for your CV to go through.

Keywords are all the skill words you see in the job description, plus others that describe requirements for the role, e.g. must have *three years' experience* in a *formal teaching role.* Note that ATS is not used by small companies (typically under 100 employees), start-ups or micro-businesses, so you can write a clever CV without clichés. A local school or church won't use ATS. Consider also that it's easier to return to work at a small organisation when you've been out for a while. Hiring practices are less formal than with large companies and government departments.

You are not trying to illustrate all the things you are good at, but trying to show that you are really good at the specific skills required for the role you are applying for. The top three to five reasons that make you suitable for the role should then appear in your covering letter or email and in the top third of your CV, usually in a 'profile' section or a 'skills' section where you list them below the profile. The body of your CV should now back up the claims you make in the covering letter and profile. In your employment history, list the responsibilities and achievements that verify the statements you have made. Likewise, only add the educational and qualification information that is relevant.

Covering the gaps

Almost everyone has gaps in their employment history. However, returning mothers often have the longest ones, ranging from two to ten or more years. Don't be discouraged, I've seen lots of women return to work after lengthy gaps. Here's what you say to cover the gap in your CV under a CAREER or EMPLOYMENT heading:

June 20??.. to Present
Career break to raise family. Utilised the time constructively to maintain and develop skills in fundraising and IT by attending a variety of courses and seminars. Currently volunteering with xxxx school PTA where I have developed leadership, minute-taking and presentation skills.

Complete the second and third sentences with your own skills and experience. Include a volunteer role (one reason it's so important) even if you just started last week. Job done!

Checklist of CV essentials

If it's been some time since you wrote a CV, here's a reminder of the essential points to get right.

- Choose a 10pt to 12pt standard font that ensures your CV is readable on the majority of computers. Use Arial, Verdana, Tahoma or Calibri, NOT Times New Roman (unless you're a lawyer).
- Black text on a white background is still seen as the optimum combination for readability but also for printing and copying.
- Have each copy of your CV proofread by a partner, friend or coach. Check for spelling, grammar and punctuation.
- Where opinions differ on correct formatting, for example whether to capitalise the first letter in a bulleted list or not, decide what format you will follow and be consistent throughout.
- Write in the third person, not the first. Do not use 'I' in your CV. That's

> You are not trying to illustrate all the things you are good at, but trying to show that you are really good at the specific skills required.

for cover letters and LinkedIn. For example "Worked as..." rather than "I worked as..."

- Your name and contact details should be on every page, in case the pages become separated after submission.
- Make sure your essential skills and experience are clearly visible to the reader, recognising that he or she may only spend seconds scanning your CV. The top third may be all that they read.
- Restrict yourself to two pages, or one if it is a summary or biography CV. Anything longer is highly unlikely to be read.
- Unless asked to do otherwise, save and submit your CV as a Word file. Some ATS systems don't read PDF format.
- Tailor every CV to the job description using keywords from the description. No blanket CVs!

The sections of a typical contemporary CV are:

Page 1

Name, Location (no need for full postal address, the city/town and first three digits of your post code will do), email address, mobile number (with answerphone)

Profile statement written in sentence format (include key words)

Skills summary in bullet points (must be keywords plus extras you think are valuable)

Employment history in reverse chronological order (month/year, name of company, your role) with descriptions including achievements

Page 2

Continue with employment history Education, professional development and memberships

Note that you don't need to list 'hobbies' or 'references available on request'. Charities and public sector roles require references and they will ask for them. In that case, you'll need to have three references ready. Choose people you trust and contact them before you make an application.

The outcome of a successful application is not a job – it's an interview. If your application has been successful you will have left your potential employer with the impression that you may be the perfect candidate. They have a document that describes what you can do and how you meet the requirements of the role. They are excited that their problem (the vacancy) is about to be solved.

> The outcome of a successful application is not a job – it's an interview.

Interviews

An interview is an opportunity for the employer and prospective employee to evaluate each other. So it's a two-way street. The employer wants to determine if the candidate will be able to perform the role and fit into the existing office culture. The candidate wants to know if the workplace suits them and if the job will provide satisfaction. So an interview can only have a positive outcome in that both parties have the chance to gather more information before coming to a more informed decision. If an employer

decides not to proceed, it does not mean the candidate has failed, only that the employer has decided that person is not right for the role. The candidate may also decide, after the interview, that this is not the job for her.

Remember, the whole selection process starts with a business problem: a vacancy that needs filling. The employer has shortlisted you because they consider it a possibility that you are the solution to the problem. You begin from a position of strength.

STAR Stories

As well as being prepared with a brief career summary story in the form of a TMAY, you'll need to answer competency-based questions such as: *"Tell me about a time you had to work with a difficult team member. What did you do?"*

The question is best answered in **STAR** format:

Situation: "When I was working at ...., my role was..."

Task: "A problem arose with ... and I was left to sort it out."

Action: "I discovered that this person was going through a difficult time with an ailing family member, so I offered to assist them by taking part of their workload."

Result: "The team improved overall and we achieved our best annual result, which was a cost efficiency of £100,000."

Make sure your result has numbers attached. Numbers communicate success in an easily understandable way (and it doesn't have to be money – some other measurable number can be substituted).

The best predictor of what you might do in future is based on what you've done in the past, so always give examples. Make sure you're the hero of the story. It's about you after all.

Be prepared

Plan your travel time to arrive early. Dress appropriately, which is one notch above what is worn by staff members on a daily basis (you may need to enquire about this with HR). Bring two copies of your CV and a notebook with 6 questions you want to ask the interviewer at the end of the interview. They may have already answered 3 during the course of the interview, so you'll have some spares ready. You can ask when you might expect to hear a result. Upon arrival, be friendly with the receptionist and everyone else you encounter. Never discuss money at the first interview. Wait for a call back before you bring up the subject.

Follow-up

After the interview, send a thank you email or a post- card addressed to a key person. You'll be remembered this way and, even if you don't get the job, you may get a call back about another position.

Wait a week and then, if you haven't heard a reply, send an email or phone them to see how things are going. If you are rejected ask for feedback. If it is given you may learn how to improve your inter- view skills. Don't expect this – but it is nice if it happens.

Try not to take rejection personally. They chose someone else because at that time they thought another candidate was more suitable. Also consider that you might be number two if the chosen candidate doesn't take the job because they've changed their mind.

Success!

When it happens you will have another meeting to discuss terms, or it may be done on the phone. This is your single best opportunity to improve their offer, by asking for more money or better working hours. This is the point where they want you so they'll be prepared to negotiate. We've seen women negotiate home work- ing for a day or two based on this princi- ple. If you're nervous about doing this, make clear that you are not threatening to withdraw, you only want to secure the right offer for the role. And congrat- ulations!

The Quick Fix

What jobs are quickly avail- able and in which sectors?

Retail. Shops are happy to take mature women for a variety of roles, but a customer- facing one could be dangerous as security levels in shops (especially small ones) are often lacking. They're watching for shoplifters, not stalkers. With admin skills, a back office role with child-friendly hours may be possible.

Hospitality. Again, front-facing could be a problem, but there are roles behind the scenes: in the office or in a restau- rant kitchen (lunch shifts for those who have cooking qualifications and child care responsibilities). Hotels always need chambermaids.

Care homes. The hours may not suit you but there are always vacancies.

Office admin. Finding an understanding temp agency may be difficult, given that roles usually run 9-5 but, having proved yourself, a full-time permanent role may be offered.

> Never discuss money at the first interview. Wait for a call back before you bring up the subject.

Julie's story

With several children and few qualifications, Julie did before-and-after school care (within the OFSTED rules) for other mums. This helped her to earn some money quickly. Then she used her network and met an estate agent who needed an answering service during school hours. Julie helped her run a virtual office. Hers was an imaginative solution to earning money and staying close to home.

 TOP TIP Returning to work after a career gap is definitely possible: networking, reviewing your CV and upgrading your skills are all doable and will lead you to success.

Notes

PART 3

HEALING AND RECOVERY AFTER LEAVING A MALE ABUSER

By Betsy de Thierry

CHAPTER 14

Supporting Children through Trauma

It can be really hard to think about the impact on your children due to the domestic abuse you have experienced. The good news, however, is that when we understand any potential effect on them a bit better, we can learn how to help them recover. In this chapter I will discuss trauma, how it affects children (and adults) and the recovery process ... but please remember not to blame yourself, and know that recovery is possible.

What is trauma?

Trauma is the result of a deeply distressing or disturbing experience(s) which can cause terror or a sense of powerlessness. When a child experiences anger in a household, whether it is explicit (aggression, violence, abuse) or when it is implicit (coercive control, manipulation, passive aggression) a child may feel terrified and powerless. Domestic abuse in the home

can cause trauma because a child's home should feel like their safest place. Domestic abuse usually stops people from feeling safe. The good news is that children can recover from the impact of this trauma when we understand more about it, and put steps in place to address it.

Children often feel powerless because they want to 'fix' the problem between the adults they love, but they realise they can't. Sadly, children also tend to blame themselves when things go wrong because they have a natural inbuilt sense that they are the centre of their world (normal and healthy for young children) so when things go wrong, they draw the conclusion that it must be their fault. This adds to their feelings of fear, therefore it can be powerful to say and repeat, in gentle conversations with them, that they are not responsible for what's happening.

> Children often feel powerless because they want to 'fix' the problem between the adults they love, but they realise they can't.

But what if they didn't see anything?

A lot of adults tell me they are certain that their child didn't see or hear the abuse, but I have found that it is amazing how much children hear and see, even if adults don't realise it. I have noticed that when I'm driving in the car, my children can't hear me when I tell them to do something, but they seem to hear every whisper that I utter to another adult! Sound familiar? Children are also impacted by the atmosphere of a home. They pick up on non-verbal atmospheres quite naturally and intuitively and can feel uneasy when adults are anxious, even when everyone is smiling! They can pick up on anger and frustration even when adults are trying to speak calmly. Children learn to 'read' adults' faces so that they can prepare for anything frightening. This is called *hypervigilance* and it can make them analyse everything you say; your body language, your facial expressions and your words. Children can become nervous and jumpy wherever they are as they learn to 'check' and 'read' adults to see what is going on.

How do we know if they are traumatised by what's happened?

Children don't often let us know *verbally* how they feel when they are frightened, it is often their *behaviour* that tells us instead. When children are scared they sometimes don't even realise that they are frightened, because coping mechanisms kick in to protect them from experiencing some of these feelings. Instead they may exhibit some of the following:

- Cry a lot
- Whine and moan more than usual
- Have anxiety issues
- Have problems with wetting, soiling
- Be irritable, restless, 'ants in their pants'
- Get angry, aggressive
- Have separation anxiety, get clingy
- Become withdrawn, they don't talk much
- Appear sad, lacking in energy, lose interest in activities
- Have friend and social problems
- Struggle to concentrate at school
- Act as if they are much younger than their actual age
- Say they hate you and love you
- Have trouble with sleeping
- Have low self esteem

This list is not exhaustive but shows the diversity of ways in which children can respond to feeling very scared.

Understanding the threat response

It can be helpful to understand the natural physiological response to threat and fear so we can understand how we ourselves may behave, and also understand some of the behaviour of our children.

A simple overview of our brain's structure can help us to understand the behaviour that is influenced by fear or terror. The brain stem, an area in our brain at the back of our head where our neck and head join, is the oldest part of the brain. When we feel fear, it makes us respond with fight (aggression, self-defensive behaviour), flight (run away, hide) or freeze (not move or become internalised) behaviours. When the brain responds with any of these immediate and instinctive reactions, it triggers many other reactions. Immediately a part of our brain called the amygdala alerts the body to the fear, the body starts pumping adrenaline and cortisol to give us enough strength to fight the threat, or run from it, or freeze like a rabbit in headlights and not move despite the threat.

Whilst this extra energy would be useful if we were confronted by a bear or lion, this extra energy can be a challenge for children to deal with when they feel ongoing fear. If they hear a door bang whilst at school or if someone drops a plate in the school canteen they may cry and run because they are reminded of an incident they heard at home. Even these small irritations can release energy and stress hormones, which means they can't sit still so they start running, wriggling, shouting, giggling, appearing aggressive or silly. They wouldn't necessarily know that they are responding to fear due to the sound of the door banging or the plate dropping. They would probably not know how they feel at all because when this instinctive reaction happens in our brain, we all immediately stop thinking rationally! This is because when the brainstem reacts to fear, and the adrenaline and cortisol are released, we struggle to use the part of our brain that is responsible for thinking rationally, and speaking. That's why, when we ask children why they reacted in a way we might perceive to have been negative, they may look blankly at us or shrug their shoulders.

It's also why we can say things or do things that seem inappropriate when we feel fear. Our prefrontal cortex (the thinking, rational, reflective brain) goes 'offline' when we feel frightened and we act instinctively. We may hide when the doorbell goes, even when we know a friend is due for coffee, or children may freeze when a teacher asks to speak to them even when they know they haven't done anything wrong. Our threat response takes over our body to try to protect us from the perceived danger.

Trauma can impact a child's body, brain, memory, emotions, relationships, learning and behaviour.

What can we do to help children when we are also traumatised or exhausted?

It is important to remember that when a child is acting instinctively because they are frightened, they are often confused by their own behaviour. We can purposely

> A simple overview of our brain's structure can help us to understand the behaviour that is influenced by fear or terror.

teach children as young as five about their brain and their automatic response to fear. That helps them feel less bad or mad! It also aids their understanding of why we, as adults, sometimes react in a way we would choose not to as well - because we have instinctive, physiological reactions to fear too!

The way to modify our instinctive reactions is to learn to catch the feelings of fear or terror before they overtake our body. Practising the following two techniques regularly (and teaching our children to practice them), when we aren't feeling frightened, can help reduce the impact of future fearful experiences and teach our body to feel safe again.

Things to do that help us heal: Breathing and Grounding

When we learn to recognise fear and start to breathe deeply and stay grounded, we can override some instinctive behaviours.

Breathing: Obviously we all breathe, but when we learn to take breaths from deep down in our diaphragm it can help reduce the physiological and emotional impact of the trauma. Try breathing in through your nose for a count of four and then breathe out deeply through your mouth. Put your hand on your tummy to make sure the breath comes from there. Younger children can enjoy lying down and putting a teddy on their tummy and feeling it drop and rise. This technique can help adults and children alike feel calmer.

> When we learn to recognise fear and start to breathe deeply and stay grounded, we can override some instinctive behaviours.

Grounding: This is a method to help the 'thinking brain' come back 'online' by noticing the fear. Sit down somewhere where your feet can feel the floor so that you are actually 'feeling the ground'. Then look for five things that are red, listen for five sounds, feel two textures nearby and notice how they feel. Do all this whilst making sure that you (and your children) are breathing deeply. If you practice this yourself and with your children when you feel fine, it can become easier to do in moments of fearfulness. It can bring a feeling of calm instead of terror.

Spending time with your children

In order for children to heal and recover from trauma, they need us to spend time with them, so it's important to choose activities that can be 'special times' that also don't exhaust us emotionally. If you enjoy cooking, choose to make some cookies with your child. If you hate cooking, don't do that activity! Make a craft, play football, tell each other jokes, have a milkshake date, go swimming etc. Find something that you can do with them that helps them to enjoy your company and feel normal. It doesn't have to take long, but try to make sure it feels fun and enjoyable. When you plan these special times to spend with your child, remember that they may not find them easy at first and could be nervous or worried. Try to be patient, they get easier. Soon the child expects to have a good time with you and feels close to you as you concentrate on them and your relationship. These times actually help the child heal from the impact of trauma and fear.

Children who have been traumatised need us to be consistent, kind and nurturing. They need us to be honest when we have made mistakes and lost patience or responded harshly. None of us are perfect, but saying sorry with our words, body language and tone of voice is really important for the children and models healthy behaviour to them. Our love and care can help them to heal.

How best to talk to children about what's happened

Children need us to be honest, but in an age-appropriate way. The language we use is really important in helping them make sense of what's happening. Something you can say to a child over four years old includes, 'I'm sorry that some-times you felt frightened about what was happening' and/or 'Would you like to talk about what has happened and what you are feeling'.

Reading story books which explore emotions or worries, can help give them the natural opportunity to talk about their feelings and worries. (There is a list of recommended books to use at the end of this chapter). It's important to give children of every age one-to-one time if possible, doing something that they enjoy with you, where they can feel loved, safe and reassured.

It's also important to help them feel they are allowed to love or like who they choose to and that no one will be cross with them and their choices. This can be really difficult and a struggle for adults to understand, but do remember that chil-

dren love their parents even when they are quite obviously behaving in horrid ways, which can surprise us adults. It is a child's instinctive response to love parental figures and when we speak to children about what has happened, we can consider explaining age appropriate facts without making them feel bad for still loving the other parent.

Different stages and ages

When children are young they may accept statements like, 'daddy was making us feel frightened and so he is not living with us now,' but they may want to ask more questions when they get older. It's important to create a culture where they can ask us, as the adult, the questions they need to ask and know that whilst we may cry or appear sad, we will prioritise their need to try and make sense of what happened. We should make the space and time to answer their questions. Children often have a habit of asking questions at the most inconvenient moment - like when you are putting them to bed and looking forward to that glass of wine, or just as you arrive at school. If you can dig deep and honour the questions and make space to let them ask you, you won't regret it. It's important that they can chat to you and feel safe to ask you questions. Just remember that they often won't talk when it fits in with our calendar and timings.

What about Christmas and birthdays and other special occasions?

These significant dates can be very stressful for many reasons but not least because the media can make us believe that these days have to be perfect. Our children can have expectations that seem impossible and families can seem perfect on social media, which can lead us to feeling guilty or like a failure. The important thing to remember is that most people feel like that, even when they appear to have money and the ideal family. Children mostly want to feel safe and cared for, and our presence with them is better than presents. Plan a few activities and trips to help relieve the pressure that can build up as big days approach. It can be a good time to ask a few friends what their best ideas are, and work out some new traditions to make memories. They don't have to be expensive but can lead to laughter and fun. The laughter doesn't devalue the emotional pain you may be experiencing, but it can help you heal as a family and make a new start. It can be a good idea, if it is at all possible, to spend time with another family or other relatives to ease some of the pressure.

When the children's behaviour creates fear in us as adults

It is not uncommon for the adult to be reminded of the abuser by aggressive behaviour that the child may show. This can indeed be triggering and challenging. Try and be honest with a friend or a therapist so that you feel less alone during these times. Talking it through with an empathetic and kind person can take some of the confusion and turmoil out of it. Having emotional support can enable you to be courageous and to breathe

> It is not uncommon for the adult to be reminded of the abuser by aggressive behaviour that the child may show.

deeply whilst you remind yourself that they are your flesh and blood and you have power to influence them with your love and kindness. You need to learn to 'catch' those internal sentences such as 'they are the same as him' and replace them with 'I have the opportunity to help them to become kind and caring'. It takes courage and patience. You need to be kind to yourself and realise that it can be hard and you probably need support.

Parenting teenagers

When we parent teenagers who are adjusting to their new family configuration following domestic abuse, it is unlikely that they will respond in a calm and reflective way. Sometimes they feel cross and angry with everyone. It can seem like they don't care about you or their siblings and only care about their friends and social life. It is a normal part of adolescent behaviour, even when children haven't grown up in abusive households, to begin to push their parents away and become more independent. It is also normal for their thinking and reflective capacity to be 'overtaken' by social relationships and emotion. Adding a change to the family dynamic at this stage in life can exacerbate these already challenging adolescent behaviours. However, teenagers do need their parents and they do need support.

It is important to remember that adolescence can be a confusing time. In some ways they are grown-up and have their own opinions but in other ways are frustratingly dependent on us and need us to help them make sense of things that are happening. The book *Trauma is Really Strange* by Haines (2015) is a good comic style book aimed at teenagers. Read it yourself first to see if it could be helpful for your teenager, then suggest they read it. If they do, it could be a good bonding exercise to debrief with them afterwards. They may find it a relief to know that their emotional and behavioural responses to the changes in the family are normal.

Teenagers worry more than they let us know and so reassuring them is important. Telling them that you love them, that you know it can be tough, that they may have questions or emotions that they need to process, all helps them feel less alone and isolated. Sometimes they may want us to text them and invite them to chat that way because it's a less intense communication style that they feel comfortable with. Planning activities that they would enjoy with you such as shopping or a sport or an activity where they can laugh and enjoy your company can build the relationship and enable everyday life to be less tense.

The general feeling of powerlessness as a parent

Parenting can often cause adults to feel exhausted and powerless, especially when the child is exerting their opinion or is angry or fussy. Even if a parent has not been traumatised, it can be challenging, but when you have survived trauma it can sometimes feel like the last straw, and that things are too tough to cope with. It takes a lot of patience to help a child learn to negotiate their feelings, opinions and desires. We need support from other adults and to be kind to ourselves. Powerlessness may well remind you of the experience of being abused or controlled and may cause you to feel overwhelmed and frightened. It's important to recognise this and do things to help you remain calm, such as the breathing technique that I mentioned previously. Sometimes the best thing to do when you are emotionally exhausted and your children are being loud and stroppy can be to pop the TV on, make a cup of tea, cry quietly, tell yourself you're doing well and breathe deeply, before joining them and being a caring parent again!

Self-care

One of the best things you can do to help your child recover from trauma is to make sure you are also taking steps to recover. When you have managed to find some support from friends or a support/community group and you have made space to process the horror of what you have experienced, you'll be able to help them more! Your way of having time and space could be having a bath each night with candles and bubbles. It could be having coffee with a supportive friend once a week or going for a walk. Choose a few things you can fit into your busy life to help you process and recover. Always remember to tell yourself that you have survived and there are beautiful things ahead for you!

TOP TIP Children may react to trauma through their behaviour. Spending time with children doing fun activities may give them opportunities to talk about their feelings which help them heal.

Notes

Further reading to help understand what to do to help traumatised children

Betsy de Thierry. (2015). *Teaching the Child on the Trauma Continuum.* Guildford: Grosvenor Publishing.

Betsy de Thierry. (2016). *The Simple Guide to Child Trauma.* London: Jessica Kingsley Publishers.

Betsy de Thierry. (2018). *The Simple Guide to Understanding Shame in Children.* London: Jessica Kingsley publishers.

Steve Haines. (2015). *Trauma is Really Strange.* London: Singing Dragon Publishers.

Daniel Siegel and Tina Payne Bryson. (2012). *The Whole-Brain Child: Twelve Proven Strategies to Nurture Your Child's Developing Mind.* New York: Delacorte Press.

Story books to read with children to help them talk and reflect on the impact of trauma

Margaret Holmes. (2000). *A Terrible Thing Happened.* Magination Press
This is great for kids aged 4-11 and can introduce to them the concept of having another person to talk to about their worries. (therapist, key worker, TA at school etc)

Jane Evans. (2014). *How are You Feeling Baby Bear. Exploring big Feelings After Living in a Stormy Home.* Jessica Kingsley Publications.
This is a useful book that helps the child explore the feelings that they can experience due to being scared. It is a perfect book to read with your child that enables them to tell you how they feel and it gives helpful ideas of how to heal.

Ali Redford. (2015). *The Boy Who Built a Wall Around Himself.* Jessica Kingsley Publications.

This book is ideal for 4-12 years (and older if you explain that you think it's a great kids book and you love it too!). It explains how sometimes the child doesn't have any feelings because they were scared but how it's important to unfreeze and let a grown up help them heal and feel again. The kind lady in the story who helps could be you or another relative or helper.

Notes

By Nikki Dhillon Keane

CHAPTER 15

Managing Mental and Physical Ill-health after Leaving

Lots of things have been written about how to understand and deal with abusive partners while you are still in the relationship, but there is much less information about how to look after yourself after you have left. If you are reading this because you are a survivor who has managed to leave an abusive partner, you will know that managing your physical and emotional health after leaving an abuser can be very challenging. When you have lived through years of abuse, you are often not used to prioritising, or even acknowledging your own needs. This chapter has some ideas about the kinds of support and self-care that can help.

Overcoming trauma after abuse

It is easy for you and others to underestimate the level of trauma that you have been through, particularly if the abuse lasted for a long time. Trauma can affect you in many different ways, causing anxiety and panic attacks, flashbacks, dissociation (a feeling of detachment from reality characterised by a wide array of experiences from mild detachment from immediate surroundings to more severe detachment from physical and emotional experiences), sleeplessness, nightmares, depression and feelings of powerlessness. Trauma can sometimes make you feel hyper-alert and dissociated or numb at other times.

The trauma of domestic abuse can affect the way you interact with the people who are supporting you, so it may be helpful to make others whom you trust aware of what you are going through. If that trauma affects you for a sustained period of time, and gets in the way of how you go about your everyday life, then it is likely that you have post traumatic stress disorder (PTSD). This is very common in survivors of domestic abuse; around 64% of abused women have PTSD[1], but help is available. One of the best kinds of therapy to help you with anxiety or PTSD is cognitive behavioural therapy (CBT). This helps you to challenge your ways of thinking and try out new behaviours which can help you to move past your trauma and reduce your anxiety. Another kind of help is eye movement desensitization and reprocessing (EMDR). This is a newer kind of therapy which has been shown to be helpful for dealing with PTSD. It helps you to process the traumatic events, keeping the useful things you have learned and discarding any unhelpful beliefs, sensations and feelings. There are links to more informa-

Depression can make you feel very isolated, so talking to other people who understand can be helpful.

tion about both of these kinds of therapy at the end of this chapter. Individual CBT and EMDR and group therapy for PTSD are available through the NHS.

Overcoming depression after abuse

Some people experience feelings of low mood after leaving an abusive relationship. It can leave you feeling physically and emotionally exhausted, with difficulty motivating yourself to do anything so that sometimes even getting out of bed in the morning is a real struggle. In some cases, feelings of low mood last only a short time and go away by themselves, but if they continue, you may have depression. Talking to a professional such as a counsellor, psychotherapist, GP or psychiatrist can help. There is information at the end of this chapter about how to access these kinds of support. As a consequence of your discussions with a professional you may also be offered antidepressant medication. There are lots of different kinds, so you can discuss with your doctor the one that is best for you. Some kinds of antidepressant medication can have side effects, like making you feel very sleepy. In many cases this is only temporary and will go away after a few weeks, but talk to your doctor if you are worried about it.

Depression can make you feel very isolated, so talking to other people who understand can be helpful. Some people find it helps to join a depression support group. For some of you, it may be more helpful to talk with other survivors of domestic abuse, either online or in person through survivor support groups, or courses like the Freedom Programme (details below).

Severe depression can lead to feelings that life is not worth living, or that you want to die. If you do have suicidal thoughts or feel that you might hurt yourself, arrange to speak to your GP urgently, who may give you a crisis number that you can call for support at any time. You can also call a 24 hour helpline such as the Samaritans (details below). If you need urgent support, you can always call 999 for an ambulance. The emergency services are there for psychological emergencies too.

Building self esteem
Another common problem that people can experience after abuse is low self esteem. When you have lived with abuse for a long time, with your perpetrator saying all sorts of horrible things about you, it can become very hard to have positive feelings about yourself. Lots of perpetrators find ways to isolate their victims from their friends and family - the people who would love and support them. Low self esteem can make you feel as though no one really cares about you, and your friends and family won't want you to get back in touch with them. Of course, family situations can be complicated, and there may be other issues going on, but in most cases, reaching out to people who love and care about you can really help rebuild your sense of self worth and help restore positive, supportive relationships. If you are having serious problems with your self-esteem,

counselling can help, but there are some other ways to help build your self-esteem:

- Write a list of your positive qualities
- Imagine how your best friend would describe you and write it down
- Ask people who care about you to tell you what they like about you
- Keep an "achievement diary" where you write down everything (even very small things) that you achieve each day. This could include everyday things like eating something healthy, getting the children to school, or doing the shopping. When you are feeling really low, even getting showered and dressed in the morning is a big achievement.

Lots of people who experience domestic abuse say that they feel as though they "lost themselves".

Finding yourself again
Lots of people who experience domestic abuse say that they feel as though they "lost themselves" while they were living with their perpetrator. This happens after years of not being free to be themselves. For some people, this feeling goes away naturally when they leave the relationship and get back in touch with family and friends who knew them from before. Things that can help you find yourself again are:

- Hobbies or activities you used to do before the abusive relationship (physical activity and pets can both be helpful in treating depression)
- Re-establishing old friendships with people who knew you before the relationship
- Wearing the kind of clothes you used to like wearing (especially if your perpetrator told you what to wear)

When you have lived for a long time with psychological and emotional abuse, it's normal for you to start to feel as though the horrible things your perpetrator says about you are true. It might feel as though a part of you believes the horrible things, but another part of you knows they are not true, which can be very confusing. A good counsellor or psychotherapist can help you to find yourself again, or to recognise and control these abusive thoughts and teach you how to keep them under control in the future.

Alcohol or drug use

Women who have been abused are three times more likely to use drugs and alcohol in problematic ways than women who have not been abused.[2] Some survivors use substances to help deal with the effects of trauma – depressants like alcohol or cannabis to deal with feeling hyper alert, and stimulants like cocaine or ecstasy to deal with feelings of numbness. These may seem helpful in the short term but can lead to long term physical and emotional problems, including dependency. If you are seeking professional help for substance use, it is important to let the practitioner know that you are a survivor of abuse so that they understand and can be sensitive to your needs. Professional treatment can range from detoxification to psychological interventions such as incentive programmes, or different kinds of therapy. If your doctor or another professional recommends couple or family therapy, it is extremely important that you tell them you are a survivor of abuse and

that it is not appropriate to include your perpetrator in your therapy.

For self-help, NICE guidelines[3] for drug misuse recommend 12 step programmes like Narcotics Anonymous. You can also get help from Alcoholics Anonymous for alcohol problems. Some alternative therapies such as acupuncture and massage are also offered for people dealing with problematic substance use.

Managing your physical health

Domestic abuse can also have long-term effects on your physical health, and managing these can be difficult. Some survivors live with the long-term injuries from physical attacks. On top of that, there are many stress–related physical conditions which result from psychological trauma. You don't have to have experienced physical abuse to have physical symptoms. Exhaustion, migraines, insomnia, stomach problems and high blood pressure are all related to stress. A range of health problems including a weakened immune system, heart disease and some cancers are associated with domestic and sexual violence. In fact, research shows that domestic abuse is the leading cause of chronic conditions and injury in women below the age of 60.[4]

If you are visiting your doctor or hospital because of a medical condition, it is important that you let her or him know that you are a survivor of abuse. Otherwise, they might not realise that your symptoms are connected to stress and

> When Women who have been abused are three times more likely to use drugs and alcohol in problematic ways.

trauma. Sometimes counselling or psychotherapy can help with stress related physical symptoms. If you find mindfulness helpful, you can join a course in mindfulness-based stress reduction (MBSR). Some different types of massage are also useful for reducing stress.

Dealing safely with your anger

You might think we are talking about perpetrators here, but in fact, most perpetrators don't really have a problem controlling their anger, they are just using their aggression as a tool to control their victim. Often, the people who really need help controlling anger are the survivors, who have probably spent years feeling justifiably angry about all the abuse they have suffered, but having no safe way to let that anger out.

When we talk about managing anger, we don't want to get rid of it all. Some anger is very positive – the kind that leads to positive things happening, like leaving a damaging relationship, helping other victims and survivors, or campaigning for changes in the law to protect victims and survivors more effectively. Other kinds of anger can be more negative – this is the kind of anger that leads to negative things happening. That doesn't just mean anger that leads someone to hurt another person, it also includes the anger with which you hurt yourself. This kind of anger

gets bottled up inside and that can lead to a range of problems:

- The anger builds up and then bursts out, uncontrolled, at the wrong person - maybe your children, your colleagues, or people trying to help you.
- The anger turns in on yourself and leads to depression, or self-harm.
- The anger gets stuck inside as recurring feelings of bitterness and negativity that only end up hurting you.

Sometimes it is a mixture of all of the above. Anger that is held in can lead to a range of physical illnesses as well as psychological and relationship problems. Anger can also lead to unhealthy rumination. It is not safe to let your anger out directly to your perpetrator, so it is important to find other ways. Some ideas of how to do this might be:

> **Anger that is held in can lead to a range of physical illnesses as well as psychological and relationship problems.**

- Writing down your angry thoughts to get them off your chest and onto paper – in a diary or in letters that you don't send, you just tear them up or burn them.
- Letting anger out through drawing or another kind of artwork
- Talking to a trusted friend or a counsellor
- Letting anger out through exercise
- Channelling it into positive anger by focussing on positive actions you can take
- Focussing on "cool" thoughts – the kind that help you calm down rather than "hot" thoughts – the kind that get you riled up

- Using visualisations to help you let go of anger, like watching your anger float away in a balloon.

You may have heard people tell you that you should forgive your perpetrator. Forgiveness is something that we can do more for ourselves than for the other person because it stops us holding onto anger and bitterness. But for some people the idea of forgiveness seems inappropriate for something as terrible as abuse. It can be easier to think more in terms of "letting go" of anger. In your mind, you can imagine handing all the pain and anger back to the person who caused it (you don't need to see them or speak to them in real life to be able to do this). As you do this you can say to yourself "I choose peace." Many therapists specialise in anger management, and if you feel that your anger is affecting your ability to function, it might be a good idea to speak to a professional.

Getting the right support
Formal therapy is not the only thing that can help you to heal. Getting back in touch with people who love you, like family and friends, can make a world of difference, especially if you have been isolated from them as a result of your abuse.

Meeting other people who have been through something similar, in a support group or online forum, can give you the opportunity to talk to people who understand what you have been through and reassure you that you are not alone.

There are support groups for issues you might be facing, e.g. depression, and also groups or courses such as the Freedom Programme where you can meet with other survivors of abuse.

Private therapy can be expensive, so if you prefer to go through the NHS, you can go to your GP and ask to be referred for talking therapy. The NHS service is called IAPT (Improving Access to Psychological Therapy) and they will give you an assessment and work out the best kind of therapy for you. You can ask about particular kinds of therapy e.g. CBT or EMDR. There is usually a waiting list for IAPT services.

There are also some domestic abuse support services which offer counselling as a part of their support. This may be free or low-cost. This is a good option because the counsellors will have training and experience in working with domestic abuse. There are links to more information below. Your local domestic abuse service should be able to give you information about specialist domestic abuse counselling in your area.

If you want to find a private counsellor or psychotherapist, the best way is to look on the BACP (British Association for Counselling and Psychotherapy) website.

Always make sure that the practitioner is registered and accredited – that means they are experienced and well-qualified. They will usually have some information about their areas of specialist knowledge, so you can look for one that has experience working with survivors of domestic abuse. It might not be written down, so when you first contact them you can ask if they have training in this kind of work. Not all qualified counsellors and psychotherapists have training in domestic abuse, so it is important to check this. Some therapists can mistake the effects of abuse for signs of other problems if they don't have the right training or awareness. There are lots of different kinds of therapy and it can be very confusing to work out which one to go for. There is some evidence that for therapy to work well, the most important thing is having a good relationship with your therapist, rather than a specific kind of therapy. So if you don't feel completely comfortable with your therapist, it might be a good idea to change and try out a different one. For survivors of abuse, it is particularly important that you feel in control of your support, so if therapy feels too directive, you can talk to your therapist about it, or find a different therapist. Sometimes you have to try a few different therapists before you find one you feel really comfortable with.

References

1 Against Violence and Abuse (AVA) Complicated Matters: A toolkit addressing domestic and sexual violence, substance use and mental ill-health (2018) p38 www.avaproject.org.uk

2 Against Violence and Abuse (AVA) Complicated Matters: A toolkit addressing domestic and sexual violence, substance use and mental ill-health (2018) p 45 www.avaproject.org.uk

3 NICE the National Institute for Clinical Excellence www.nice.org.uk

4 Kahrmel Wellness "The Impact of Domestic Violence and Abuse" (2014) www.kahrmelwellness.com

Where to get support and information

For urgent support:
Samaritans:
Website: www.samaritans.org for more information or your local branch to visit
Helpline: 08457 90 90 90 (free from any phone 24 hours a day)
Email: jo@samaritans.org

For more information about different kinds of talking therapies:
NHS talking therapies
Webpage: www.nhs.uk/conditions/stress-anxiety-depression/benefits-of-talking-therapy

Domestic Violence UK (NHS)
Webpage: domesticviiolenceUK.org/nhs-post-can-i-get-free-therapy-or-counselling

Women's Aid information on emotional support
Webpage: www.womensaid.org.uk/the-survivors-handbook/emotional-support-and-counselling/

British Association for Counselling and Psychotherapy (BACP)
Website: www.bacp.co.uk for information about different kinds of counselling or to find a private practitioner

British Association for Behavioural and Cognitive Therapies
Website: www.babcp.com click on "public" for more information about CBT or to find a private practitioner

EMDR Institute
Website: www.emdr.com for more information about EMDR or to find a private practitioner

For more information about Mindfulness:
NHS information about mindfulness
Webpage: www.nhs.uk/conditions/stress-anxiety-depression/mindfulness/

For peer or group support for domestic abuse:
The Freedom Programme
Website: www.freedomprogramme.co.uk a course which teaches about domestic abuse in a group with other survivors or online if there isn't a local one for you

Restored Online Network

Restored online network for Christian Survivors of Domestic abuse. Contact info@restoredrelationships.org for more information or to join this community

....

For support for problematic drug and alcohol use:
NHS information on addiction
Webpage: www.nhs.uk/live-well/healthy-body/addiction-what-is-it/

Alcoholics Anonymous
Website: www.alcoholics-anonymous.org.uk for more information or to find a meeting
Helpline: 0800 9177 650
Email: help@aamail.org

Narcotics Anonymous
Website: www.ukna.org including local group finder
Helpline: 0300 999 1212 (10am to midnight)

Notes

By Faye Hurley

CHAPTER 16

Focusing on Self-Care / Self-Worth

I grew up in an abusive home, my parents were a church minister and wife, and later I became a Christian woman who left her own abusive husband. So I can sympathize with what you have been through, and how you're feeling right now.

I had been told that I needed to "pray more" for my husband, and that "God doesn't condone divorce"; as well as "your children need to have their Dad around, you'll ruin their lives if you leave". So the decision to finally leave was one of the hardest I'd ever made. I believed that I was going against God, that I wasn't a *real* Christian, that I wouldn't be going to Heaven, that I was a bad Mum, and a very selfish woman.

I later came to realise, with the help of *Restored*, that what I was asked to accept were lies, fed to me through a church, its leaders and members, that were based on a combination of misogyny, patriarchy and misunderstanding.

I also came to understand that the critical thoughts and feelings I had about myself were collectively termed as 'shame'. **Shame sits at the entirely opposite end of the scale to self-worth.**

A well-known expert on shame, Brené Brown, in her TED talk entitled: 'Listening To Shame' says:

"Shame drives two big tapes in your mind: "[You're] Never good enough" and "Who do you think you are?" Shame is not guilt. Shame is a focus on self. I am bad. I'm sorry I am a mistake. Guilt is about behaviour. I did something bad. I'm sorry I made a mistake"

During my abusive relationship and afterwards – until I began to rebuild my self-worth – I felt completely enveloped in shame. I believed I was wrong, bad, selfish, evil, greedy, stupid, ugly, useless; and that I **didn't deserve** to *have* what I wanted, or to be *loved* in the way I wanted. This is **shame**. This is **unworthiness**.

At that time, I had no idea that those shameful beliefs had been imposed on me by other people who had their *own*, deep rooted, self-worth issues. In a misguided attempt to make themselves feel better and more powerful, they were now trying to project their own feelings of shame onto me.

I had no idea that the beliefs I'd adopted from them were **not** from God – and were certainly **not** what He'd ever said, felt or believed about me.

What Is Self-Worth & Where Does It Come From?
Our self-worth is our belief in our inherent value as a human being; worthiness is our birthright. The very fact that we have

been *created* by God and therefore *exist*, means we are worthy. We *never* have to strive or work hard to earn or prove our worth, our inherent value.

If I were to ask you to stand in a maternity ward, and look around at all of the babies in their cribs, and ask you *"Which of these babies are worthy and valuable, and which are not?"*, you would immediately tell me *"They all are"*. These babies do not need to prove their value before they deserve to be loved and receive what they need and want, and neither do you.

You already understand this truth, deep within you, the truth of *your* inherent value, without the need to prove yourself or earn it – but somewhere along your life's journey, other people have made you doubt it. That doesn't change the **truth**, which is that you have *always* been and *will* always be worthy.

> Our worthiness has come from God, the One who created us, and it is rooted in unconditional love.

Our worthiness has come from God, the One who created us, and it is rooted in **unconditional love**.

Shame, on the other hand, is rooted in **conditional love**; or put another way, "love" which has conditions placed upon it – e.g. you must be the perfect wife/daughter/mother/friend, you must not express anger (that's not Christian, or feminine!), you must always place others' needs before your own, you must be (constantly) kind, you must keep up appearances, you must not have different opinions from those held by your church or family (...and the list goes on). If you meet these conditions, **then** you will be loved and accepted.

And what is the alternative? If you do not meet these conditions, you will be shamed, unloved and abandoned. To be abandoned is one of the greatest fears of all human beings - so you can see the power that shame truly has to control us, and the power and control that those who use shame as a tool have over us.

However, just as God's love is unconditional, the more that we *unconditionally* love ourselves, the more we break away from the power that shame (unworthiness) has over us.

You can see that by doing this, once again, we are returning to the pattern of **conditional love** for ourselves, rather than **unconditional**.

The world invites us to live like this; negatively comparing ourselves, so that we end up feeling shameful – it's big business! Believing that we have to compete against others in order to be enough, be worthy and to feel good about ourselves, leaves us feeling separate from others, separate from God, and alone.

The antidote is always to return to the truth of your inherent self-worth, by using unconditional self-love, also known as *self-compassion*.

The difference between self esteem and self worth, is that self worth comes from within us.

What Is Self-Esteem & Where Does It Come From?

Self-esteem is related to **how much you like yourself**. If you hold someone in 'high esteem', it means that you like them, you respect them, and value them – and the same can be applied to ourselves with the term 'self-esteem'.

However, the difference between self-esteem and self-worth, is that self worth comes from **within us** (internal/intrinsic) whereas self-esteem comes from **outside of us** (external). We base our self-esteem upon **comparisons** with other people. We look at other people's beauty, skills, achievements, knowledge, relationships and *opinions of us,* and then place a value upon ourselves dependent on how well (or not) we 'measure up'.

What Is Self-Confidence & Where Does It Come From?

It is interesting to note that it is possible to *appear* self-confident, yet have little or no self worth; in fact many of my clients are like this. You can also see it every day within the media – so many talented, wealthy celebrities, who appear to be uber-confident, struggle with addictions, bankruptcy, suicidal thoughts and so on.

People ask *"Why do they have these issues, when they have such a perfect life and seem so confident?"* The answer is that, deep down, they don't believe they are enough; deep down they believe they are **unworthy**.

Self-worth leads to true self-confidence.

The knowledge that you are just as worthy,

and valuable, and important as every other person on the planet and that you have been given *unique* skills, passions, talents and abilities that the world needs, will always lead you to feeling *truly* self-confident.

What Is Self-Care & Why Is It Important?

Many people mistakenly believe that 'self-care' means pampering yourself. Whilst 'pampering' can be *included* within self-care (should you wish), it certainly is not the entirety of it!

I'd like you to think of someone, right now, that you care deeply for – perhaps that would be your child(ren), your parent, your best friend etc – and think about the answer to this question "What do you do to show you care for them...what is included?" I can guarantee your answer will not be just "pampering them"!

When you care for someone deeply, you speak kindly to them, you encourage them, you praise them, you support them emotionally and physically, you hug them, you tell them you love them (and many other things)...isn't that right? The same needs to go for you. You have experienced some extremely challenging and traumatic events. If someone you cared for had experienced something similar, what would you recommend they do? For my clients, the first thing I recommend is to get support, and to begin healing.

Healing isn't pretty, but it's healthy. You need to surround yourself with empathetic people who understand what

you've been through, and who will listen to you and encourage you to express yourself – the good, bad and ugly. Expressing your feelings of repressed anger (*one of the biggest areas of my work*) as well as deep sadness/grief/loss, guilt and shame will enable you to heal and move forward. And later, when you feel ready, you will begin to reclaim your power and self-worth even further by restoring your personal boundaries, asking for what *you* want and giving *your-self* **permission to receive.**

But doing all of these things requires **energy**. And that is exactly why putting self-care into practice is **absolutely vital** for you. Self-care is the **physical demonstration** of self-love; and it is essential for your physical, emotional and mental well-being, as well as for a healthy and happy life for you.

Isn't Self-Care Selfish?

One of the greatest challenges I face with my clients is undoing their belief that self-care is selfish, and this belief can run very deep with women of faith. As the daughter of a church minister myself, and growing up in church environments for the majority of my life, I can understand where this belief has come from, and why it is so hard to let go of it.

Within my own religion, I was covertly, and sometimes overtly, taught that asking for/having/giving myself what I really *want* was greedy, selfish and prideful, and therefore made me a bad person, woman and Christian. I have worked with women who were even taught that their desire to

Healing isn't pretty, but it's healthy.

133

be wealthy, for example, meant that they wouldn't go to Heaven. You can certainly see why so many women feel not only guilty, but actually *fearful*, of putting self care into practice!

The fact that we know Jesus had a 'servant's heart' and sacrificed himself for us/others seems to have translated itself, within Christian homes, as meaning we must also sacrifice ourselves by putting the needs of others before our own – and this is especially prevalent for women.

> Do you think that you are better able to give to (serve) others when you are rested and fulfilled, or when you are tired and resentful?

But let me ask you to answer this question truthfully – *do you think that you are better able to give to (serve) others when you are rested and fulfilled, or when you are tired and resentful?*

A commonly used example to demonstrate this principle is using an oxygen mask on a plane. In order to take care of others, you must first put on your own oxygen mask. With my clients, I often use the adage **"You cannot serve from an empty vessel"**. Remember, even Jesus took time away from his disciples, purely to replenish *himself* – and if it's ok for Him, it's good enough for you too!

Selfishness would be to deny other people the right to self-care, but that is not what you would be doing. You understand that everyone, including yourself, has the God-given right to demonstrate self love, by practising self-care; and that in doing so the people around you also reap the benefits, because you are then able to *joyfully give* from your 'overflow', rather than the scrapings from the bottom of your barrel!

How Can I Put Self-Care Into Practice?

Self-care includes *anything* that helps to restore you, replenish you and re-energise you; and that can mean different things for different people - there is no wrong way to do it, you simply do what makes **you** feel good! It is highly likely that you have spent the majority of your life putting the needs of others before your own, and therefore self-care will be quite an 'alien concept' for you – so I'd like to offer you some of my own suggestions which have had the greatest impact upon my clients.

1) Reach out for support

You are not alone. Connect with empathetic people – professionals, friends etc. Don't forget, shame *disconnects* us and worthiness *connects* us. Never underestimate the power of surrounding yourself with those who love and care for you, while you are learning to love and care for yourself.

Self-care includes anything that helps to restore you, replenish you and re-energise you

2) Express your thoughts and feelings

It is *healthy* for you to express your thoughts and feelings, and to do so brings healing. You are a human being who has the right to feel and express anger, grief, guilt, shame in appropriate ways – such as with a professional counsellor, therapist, or trusted friend.

Not expressing them does not make those thoughts and feelings go away, it only represses them – which can lead to damaging behaviours, as well as physical, emotional and mental health issues. Jesus expressed anger and grief; use Him as your example.

3) Become your own best friend or loving parent

Throughout this chapter, you can see that self-judgement and criticism are at the core of shame. The only way to overcome this is to use loving, praising and kind language towards yourself on a *consistent* basis.

One of the most powerful exercises I give my clients is to find a childhood photo of themselves and to look at that photo each time they begin to self-criticise, because it is virtually impossible to continue with the criticism whilst looking at the innocent 'child self'. I also ask my clients to put that same photo somewhere they will see it every day and literally *speak out* loving, kind, encouraging words to the 'child self'.

It often feels clunky and unnatural, and even silly at first, but over time it becomes familiar – your 'new normal'. I encourage you to do the same – perhaps using some of the words and phrases that God says about you within the Bible.

4) Forgive yourself

My clients are often their own worst 'inner bully' and struggle with forgiving themselves for getting into an abusive relationship, for not leaving sooner and/or for 'allowing' their children to experience what they did.

The abuse you and your children endured was **not your fault**.

So, in line with the above points, I encourage you to share your guilt and shameful (critical) thoughts with a trusted person and, with their support and encouragement, find it within yourself to forgive yourself, so that you can move on to receive the beautiful future you deserve.

5) Decide what you want and make it 'non-negotiable'

If you've ever heard of the term 'personal boundaries' this is what it means – deciding what **you** want (and how **you** want to be treated) and never settling for anything less.

Setting and asserting personal boundaries was the thing that caused the greatest transformation in my own life, and it is the same for the women I now work with. I often say, if I was only allowed to teach one thing, it would be boundaries. (Please see Chapter 17: *Boundaries and Healthy Relationships* for a further discussion).

When you feel strong enough, write a list of all the things that have caused you anger and hurt, and then think about which 'right' of yours was denied. For example, if your partner did not allow you to express you own opinion without consequences, then your human right to have and express your own opinion without fear was denied.

Once you have a list of these 'denied rights', create your own 'Personal Bill Of Rights' by writing them in this format:
"I have the right to have, and express, my own opinions without fear"
"I have the right to....be treated with respect, to have fun, to be loved etc.....(fill in the blanks)"

Your newly created 'Personal Bill Of Rights' can now define your **boundaries**. These are therefore non-negotiable, in order to build the **life you want**. The more you stick to these and assert them, the more you reclaim your self-worth and begin living the life you want.

6) Daily self-care

Write a list of things you have loved to do in your past (including your childhood), and would love to do in your future. Let your mind wander and your pen flow! Next, write at least one of these things on your calendar/diary/phone to **actually do** that week. It doesn't matter how big or small that thing is – coffee with a friend, having a sleep when your baby sleeps during the day, going for a walk or swim, reading a book, getting a massage...anything you like! The point is, you are beginning to send yourself two strong messages that will completely change your life – "I Am Worthy", and "I Am Worthy To *Receive*!"

Self-care is the external sign of your *internal* self-love transformation – and it breathes *joy* back into your life!

Self care is the external sign of your internal self love transformation – and it breathes joy back into your life!

And Finally....

What I've shared with you in this chapter is the exact information that transformed my own life, and continues to do so for my clients. When I took my children and fled my marriage, my ex husband told me that I would "end up back in the gutter where I came from". Yet here I am – in a healthy relationship for the last 10 years with a man who loves me and my children, and I've become an award-winning entrepreneur who runs a successful business. I am also realising my dream – playing my part in journeying with women and children who have experienced abuse.

God has a beautiful plan for your life too and I'm here to rekindle your hope and faith in that. Your intrinsic worth comes from and is given to you by God, but you also have *free will* to choose whether to **believe it, and to live in accordance with it**.

So I encourage you today to make a promise to yourself, to release the old, shameful beliefs about your lack of worth – which were never truly yours - and to step back into your divine worthiness.

You are inherently good, worthy, and lovable – and always will be.

Return to self love. Return to your rightful place as God's daughter. Receive the life and love you truly deserve.

TOP TIP   Self-care is not greedy, selfish or prideful; it is healthy and appropriate self-love that restores, replenishes and re-energises you.

Notes

By Esther Sweetman

CHAPTER 17

Boundaries and Healthy Relationships

Christians often applaud self-sacrifice and unselfish behaviour but this can lead to an unhealthy lack of self-care and self-respect. When we have lived with an abuser, we have typically learnt to put the needs and desires of others first, and struggle to re-assert ourselves without guilt or shame. We need to re-learn the importance of developing our own personal boundaries, the healthy pursuit of fulfilling our wants and needs and understanding our own limits.

What are boundaries?

Personal boundaries are guidelines, rules or limits that we create to identify reasonable, safe and permissible ways for other people to behave towards us and how we will respond when someone passes those limits. Boundaries are non-negotiable lines we set to feel comfortable in a friendship or relationship. If we decide in advance about how we might respond when these lines are crossed, it will enable us to uphold our boundaries. Thinking about and setting boundaries can protect us from further harm and ensure healthy relationships. Boundaries keep what is important to us and our values at the forefront of any relationship and keep our self-respect intact. Setting boundaries is an important element of self-care.

Cloud and Townsend (2017, 2000) have written many good books on boundaries which can be broken down into discrete categories:

Physical - no one should touch you in a way that hurts you or makes you uncomfortable.

Emotional - your feelings are valid and you are responsible for them and not for someone else's feelings. No one can tell you how to feel.

Material - sharing material belongings is up to you.

Spiritual - your beliefs are yours and sharing them is up to you. Neither do you need to feel pressured by others to believe a certain way.

Mental - your thoughts and opinions are valid and should be respected.

Examples of Boundaries

So what exactly does a boundary look like? Boundaries are simple concepts and phrases that describe our limits, tolerances and expectations; they communicate who we are and what we want or require from a partner, friend or church or family member. Eg:

- Expect respect from others and not constant criticism, even when made in jest.
- Expect others not to pressure you into agreeing to things you don't want to do or say.
- Expect reliability and kindness from others and not accept inconsistent treatment.

Expressing our boundaries to others - *Finding our Voice*

Having an assertive attitude rather than a passive or aggressive stance is the best way to communicate boundaries. Using appropriate body language, eye contact, facial expression and voice level can all help in expressing one's own boundaries well.

Domesticshelter.org[1] have written about the need to rediscover your voice and re-learn how to express yourself so that you can thrive and engage in a healthy relationship. They suggest a few ways to do this.

- *List your favourites* - start listing what your favourites are in all areas: movies, songs, meals - understand that your preferences are valid.
- *Consider your vision* - what do you want your life to look like? What do you want a relationship to look like?
- *Take up more space* - carry your head high, look people in the eye, practise confident body language.
- *Start using more 'I' statements* - 'I would like . . .' - your needs and desires are valid.
- *Practise speaking up* - your thoughts and opinions are important.
- *Find what makes you happy* - what gives you joy - pursue that!

Considering Elements of a Healthy Relationship

We all know the key elements of a good relationship: respect, honesty and good

communication. Most people think those elements are in place when they enter a relationship or get married. Yet we also know that just because a person demonstrates respect, honesty and good communication skills in their working life, for example, it does not necessarily mean that this is how that same person will behave in an intimate relationship.

So this discussion will challenge us to consider **observable predictors**, not just individual traits, when thinking about healthy long-term relationships and to be able to identify **red flags** that may be causes for concern.

Know your worth - review your expectations, values and boundaries.

An intimate relationship is not necessary to create a fulfilled and purposeful life. However, I think some aspects of the following discussion on healthy relationships can be equally applied to our friendships and even to our own behaviour.

The following are a few key ingredients or potential predictors of long-term healthy relationships:

Taking emotional and behavioural responsibility demonstrates maturity and is required to build healthy friendships or relationships - i.e. taking responsibility for one's own feelings, actions, needs and happiness. If your partner/ friend is dependent on you to 'fix' any part of their world, or blames you for the way they are feeling or behaving, this is a **red flag**. Similarly, we cannot go into a relationship hoping that this person will be the '*solution*' to our problems.

Being willing to support each other's goals and achievements. In healthy relationships no one is threatened or jealous of each other's talents, skills, intelligence or achievements. There should be mutual encouragement and support for each other's endeavours and mutual celebration for each other's successes.

Learning from and respecting differences. Differences and even conflict are accepted as an inevitable part of social interactions and are not to be feared but are viewed as opportunities to learn and grow together. Being able to listen attentively and to respect each other's point of view and not always having to be right or win an argument is key. The focus should be on respecting differences in opinions and beliefs, and not controlling them.

Feelings are seen as acceptable and can be shared openly, honestly and respectfully. There are not good and bad feelings but only better and worse ways of expressing them. For example, anger is an acceptable feeling but it is not acceptable to express it in a threatening, injurious or harmful manner or when it becomes the predominant feeling expressed.

Are there any deal-breakers?

Know your worth - review your expectations, values and boundaries. Being able to clearly articulate what you feel are acceptable and unacceptable behaviour and attitudes towards money, time, family, core values etc and understanding what your partner's are is vital. **Do they align?** Decide what you will accept and

will not accept before entering a relationship and then don't compromise on these key issues. Compromise is for issues that are not central.

Don't dismiss any early concerns you have - discuss them. Don't project your values onto your partner. That is, don't assume your partner thinks like you, just because they are a Christian. Some perpetrators of domestic abuse, for example, are Christians - it doesn't mean that you will hold the same values in regards to respect, consideration, kindness, shared responsibility, emotional maturity and equality.

Be prepared to leave the relationship respectfully if things are not right.

Be prepared to leave the relationship respectfully if things are not right.

How to manage friends, family, church leaders and church members who blame us, side with or collude with the abuser, actively remain neutral or are unsupportive.

Experiencing domestic abuse is horrific and the strength needed to leave an abuser is huge. Often the perpetrator continues abusing even after we leave. Experiencing no support from friends, family or church leaders and members can often feel like another assault. Sometimes this lack of support can come from ignorance and sometimes the individuals have actively chosen to 'remain neutral' or to take the abuser's side. Sometimes these individuals may be equally fearful of the abuser and just do not want to take a stand that might create conflict with them.

No matter what the reason, we need to make a decision as to whether the influence of this person (people) in our lives is hurting us more than helping us. If they are simply ignorant of the circumstances, then we can choose to be vulnerable (if we feel safe enough to do so) and open up to them about what has really happened, thereby helping them to understand what they could do to support us.

If judgemental and hurtful words or actions are still forthcoming, then just as you might have had to do with your abuser, consider separating yourself from this person/people - this might be the healthiest choice. This can be difficult as they might be family members, long time friends or your church community.

Only you will be able to decide whether your recovery would progress better without them in your life. Or you may need space from them for a period of time. You can then put the effort you would have invested in that friendship, into making new friends and community who are more supportive. There is no doubt that this is difficult, but it may come as a relief to realise that we do not need to accept poor treatment from others, even if they have previously been close to us. Finding individuals to befriend who have values more closely aligned with your own may be a better use of your time and energy.

The main point to remember is that if you choose to separate yourself from someone, do not become isolated. Reach out to others who have the capacity to support you.

References

1 **Domestic Shelters.org** (2016) *Express Yourself: Learning to find your voice again after escaping an abusive relationship can take work.* (Accessed on 05/11/18) www.domesticshelters.org/domestic-violence-articles-information/express-yourself#.V-kiKZMrKi4

Henry Cloud, John Townsend. (2017). ***Boundaries: When to say Yes and when to say No - To Take Control of your Life.*** Michigan: Zondervan Publishing.

Henry Cloud, John Townsend. (2000). ***Boundaries in Dating: How Healthy Choices Grow Healthy Relationships: Making Dating Work.*** Michigan: Zondervan Publishing.

TOP TIP Know your boundaries before you enter a relationship so that you will more easily be able to uphold them when someone crosses a line.

Notes

By Miriam Hargreaves

CHAPTER 18

Dealing with Sexual Exploitation in Relationships

What is sexual exploitation?

In your marriage or relationship, have you been forced or manipulated to:

* engage in sexual acts you are uncomfortable with or which are physically painful?
* have sex when you really didn't want to?
* have regular sex when your spouse has been abusing and controlling you in other ways and manipulated you into having sex in order to 'kiss and make up?'
* act or look a certain way that leaves you feeling used – or have you been criticised for the way you are in bed or called 'frigid' or 'vanilla'?
* had sex withheld as a tool to make you comply?
* have sex with people your spouse knows for money or have been 'passed around' his friends?
* be involved in prostitution?

Maybe you have been told or thought:

* it's not abuse when you are married, because it is a wife's duty to have sex when her husband wants.
* if I just do what he wants then he will

be happier and nicer afterwards.

- if I just do what he wants then the threats and abuse might stop, at least for a bit.
- he's often sad and sorry after he has treated me badly and the Bible tells us we have to forgive.
- I don't feel brave enough or strong enough any more to say 'no'.
- no one at church would have a clue and I don't know how I would tell anyone.

Sexual Exploitation in a Relationship

Sexual exploitation in a marriage or relationship often develops over time. Abuse starts with the abuser using little forms of control: belittling, criticism, taking away freedom bit by bit. The same experience can occur regarding control around sex, as the sexual relationship is not a separate thing from the rest of the marriage. Scott Miller, a domestic abuse specialist says, "There is a great deal of sexual violence that happens, so you get this guy who believes he can dominate the partner, beat her into submission; as one of my colleagues often says, that kind of behaviour, that kind of thinking doesn't stop at the bedroom door."

Sexual exploitation and abuse occur as one expression among many, when one partner exerts control and domination over another, in an intimate relationship.

The World Health Organisation defines sexual violence as:

"Any sexual act, attempt to obtain a sexual act, unwanted sexual comments or advances, or acts to traffic, or otherwise directed, against a person's sexuality using coercion, by any person regardless of their relationship to the victim, in any setting, including but not limited to home and work." This includes: rape, sexual assault, sexual harassment/ bullying, sexual exploitation (coercion and exploitation in the sex industry) and trafficking.

Sexual Exploitation for Money

Many women who have been sexually exploited speak of how it happened gradually. A relationship that may have started romantically with the hope of security and companionship, in time, may have changed and become abusive.

Sexual exploitation does not happen to 'a certain kind of woman.' The numbers of women involved in selling sex in the UK are estimated at around 73,000 (UK House of Commons Report on Prostitution 2016). Many women contact 'Beyond Support' (see below), the phone support service run by Beyond the Streets, a charity for women involved in the sex industry who want to find routes out. These are women who would never have dreamed that they could end up selling sex. Women can find themselves being used in this way through different routes and from different backgrounds.

Maybe you haven't been 'sold' by a partner, but receiving money or favours for sex is the same abuse of power and broken trust. One survivor wrote, "If I wanted to

> Abuse starts with the abuser using little forms of control: belittling, criticism, taking away freedom bit by bit.

Domestic Abuse Intervention Project Duluth, MN www.duluth-model.org

VIOLENCE

PHYSICAL / SEXUAL

USING COERCION AND THREATS
Making and/or carrying out threats to do something to hurt her • threatening to leave her, to commit suicide, to report her to welfare • making her drop charges • making her do illegal things.

USING INTIMIDATION
Making her afraid by using looks, actions, gestures • smashing things • destroying her property • abusing pets • displaying weapons.

USING ECONOMIC ABUSE
Preventing her from getting or keeping a job • making her ask for money • giving her an allowance • taking her money • not letting her know about or have access to family income.

USING EMOTIONAL ABUSE
Putting her down • making her feel bad about herself • calling her names • making her think she's crazy • playing mind games • humiliating her • making her feel guilty.

POWER AND CONTROL

USING MALE PRIVILEGE
Treating her like a servant • making all the big decisions • acting like the "master of the castle" • being the one to define men's and women's roles

USING ISOLATION
Controlling what she does, who she sees and talks to, what she reads, where she goes • limiting her outside involvement • using jealousy to justify actions.

USING CHILDREN
Making her feel guilty about the children • using the children to relay messages • using visitation to harass her • threatening to take the children away.

MINIMIZING, DENYING AND BLAMING
Making light of the abuse and not taking her concerns about it seriously • saying the abuse didn't happen • shifting responsibility for abusive behavior • saying she caused it.

VIOLENCE

PHYSICAL / SEXUAL

buy something or go somewhere with girlfriends or wanted him to do something for me – he'd say – I'll give you ££ to do that if you will have sex."

Sex and Porn Addiction

Perhaps his obsession with sex is taking over his life and he is abusing you in his addiction. Addiction to sex is any sexual behaviour that feels out of control, and becomes harmful to yourself or others. 27,000 people google 'sex and porn addiction' every day. (Paula Hall Clinical Director of Laurel Centre, Ted Talk 2016). Sex and porn addiction is like any addiction: a cycle starts where sex is used to numb emotional pain, or loss of control. There is a brief 'relief' of acting on those feelings but then the guilt and shame of using porn or using and abusing someone to get sex occurs. These feelings of guilt and shame can then be taken out abusively on a partner. Sex becomes the drug, leading to guilt and shame, leading to abusive behaviour which starts the cycle again with emotional pain.

For the addict, there is a drive to find sex wherever possible, so that can include:

- pushing a partner for sex far more often and in ways that become abusive
- cheating on a partner through affairs, paying for sex with other people, sexting others, or 'one-offs'
- using porn, webcam sex and masturbation and perhaps forcing that on a partner
- sexual abuse of under 18s

If you are in a relationship with someone who is using sex as a drug, then it may be that secrecy and shame stop you from reaching out for help. If he is having sex with other people, it is not because there is something wrong with you, it is because he is making unhealthy choices. Infidelity is abuse of a partner. (Please refer to Chapter 19: *Infidelity and its link to Domestic Abuse* and Chapter 20: *Pornography and its link to Domestic Abuse* in this handbook for further discussion on these topics.)

> **If he is having sex with other people, it is not because there is something wrong with you, it is because he is making unhealthy choices**

Karen and Phil

'Karen' and 'Phil' knew a lot of people through work, church and the school gate. His friends often came to their house for beers to watch sport on TV at the weekend. In time, the TV nights got longer and the drinking heavier. Phil did not want Karen to go out with her friends. Sometimes he got very angry and hit her so she stayed in. She felt uncomfortable but she thought, 'if you can't beat them, join them' so she would have a drink with them all. One night, the conversation turned personal about her. One guy paid her 'compliments' but it didn't stop there and Phil started to joke, saying "Help yourself mate, if you're keen". He knew that before they were married, she had slept with different men. He was critical about her life before and when he started demanding things in their sex life that she did not like, he would say "You're an experienced woman of the world. Why are you acting so innocent now?"

He demanded more and more, became angrier and physically aggressive and threatened to leave her and the children if she said 'no.'

One Saturday night after the football, he pulled her down to sit next to a friend. He said he had asked if she wanted to 'make things interesting' with his friend. She laughed and said 'not really!' Phil whispered, 'If you know what's good for you, you'll give him what he's asking for.' Phone messages started from the friend and Phil became more aggressive. Finally, out of fear for the family and because she thought 'if I do it once then he'll stop,' she agreed to it.

Soon the friend came round regularly. She found a message on Phil's phone one day that showed her that money was passing hands. How had it come to this? It felt like living two lives, the public one and the private shame and dread with constant fear that someone would find out. She so wanted help but the idea of telling their pastor or his wife made her feel ill. She did not know where to turn. Phil's Sunday morning church face was so different from his Saturday night one and people liked and respected him at church.

Maybe you have experienced something like this or survived other kinds of bad treatment around sex in your relationship.

The first step to recovery is to know that this is abuse, and to recognise that you did not cause it, that you are not the problem. Secondly, it is important to understand that you can't change your partner. Thirdly, know you have survived something traumatic and you are the one who knows best what you need when looking for help. You are not alone and finding the right support is very important.

You may be in denial yourself that what is happening constitutes abuse. It is important to be clear here that when you are coerced or forced into doing something sexually that you do not want to do then this is abuse. It can constitute a crime.

Who Can I Talk To and Will It Help?

In some churches sex and abuse are not talked about. It might even feel that Christian friends are the hardest people to go to when you are facing sexual abuse. We can be left feeling isolated and ashamed, especially where teaching on sex is more about sin and less about compassion and understanding of what it is like to be controlled through sex.

Christian teaching can be used negatively and male leadership/control can mean that women are expected to submit.

When it comes to sexual exploitation and abuse, some Bible verses have been used to teach that a woman should never deprive her husband of sex (1 Corinthians 7:4). It says that 'The wife gives authority over her body to her husband.' Two points to note here are:

1   It also says, 'The husband gives authority over his body to his wife.' The sexual relationship is to be mutual and equal.
2   Each partner 'gives' authority, it is not taken from them.

You may know that your pastor has been understanding and supportive of others in similar situations. Or, you may suspect that they won't understand because you have seen how they have dealt with other situations. The teaching that you have heard in your church will give you an idea of their views. In some churches, people are expected to turn only to Christian agencies and not secular ones. However, there are a lot of good secular organisations with a lot of experience in supporting survivors of abuse.

Finding the Right Person

If it does not look as if someone in leadership in your church is going to be the best person, then think about who could be a good listener. Your church should have a Safeguarding Advisor with whom you could speak. It may be someone who has shown you signs that they are good at listening and not judging.

Seek counselling to help you process what you have gone through. You may not

> You may be in denial yourself that what is happening constitutes abuse.

think that you need help or support but it is worth the investment of time to discuss what you have experienced and work through putting in place new boundaries to keep yourself safe. Looking for a counsellor is not you saying that you are the problem; it is just a way of finding some focussed, confidential support. It may help to interview a counsellor before you decide if they are appropriate for you. Questions to ask: Have you been trained in domestic abuse? Have you had previous clients who have experienced domestic abuse?

You can also ask a counsellor if they use a 'gender and trauma-informed approach'. If they suggest couples counselling, you will then know it would be best to look for someone else, as couple counselling in this situation is not appropriate. This is not a relationship or marriage issue. This is a domestic abuse issue where the abuser needs to be held to account for his behaviour. This does not occur during couple counselling.

Recovery is about seeking the right professional and community support.

The pathway to recovery from sexual abuse can take different turns. Once you have talked about it and have found some understanding and support, it can feel so much better. However, the physical, emotional and mental effects of what you have been through are very real and recovery can take time, years in some cases. Don't let that stop you starting on the path to recovery and getting the help and support you need now.

It is normal to feel shame, and that you have somehow lost your sense of who you really are. You have been forced to live a lie and do things that you didn't choose to do or never thought you would do. Your beliefs about the woman you are can feel separated and covered over by what you feel you have become, what you feel that God thinks about you, what you think about God (e.g. where was He?) and what you have been told you are by your abuser.

Those beliefs can be powerful. You are not wrong to feel hurt, angry and confused. Our sexuality and our sense of who we are, are tied up together in a deep way. When you feel broken up inside by sexual abuse, recovery is about seeking the right professional and community support and trusting that God loves you and that you are a woman of worth.

The truth is that whatever has happened, you are a person of value. You are loved by God, no matter what has happened. You are still loved by God. You are precious to God. Nothing and no one else can change this. You have survived trauma and that trauma does not have to follow you forever. Someone you trusted has done and said things that can bring a great sense of shame. It tells us the lie that bad things that happen are proof that you are not good enough. However, God made us good enough, has taken away our shame and sees us as valuable, lovable and worthy of a better future. That's what the 'double portion' is in Isaiah 61:7.

If God does not feel close, this does not have to be forever. Receiving support and understanding from others is an important part of being put back together. If you can, talk to God, He can take your anger, hurt and pain. God loves you. Tell Him about your pain.

Staying Healthy after Sexual Exploitation and Abuse

If you suspect or know that your partner has had sex with someone else, or if you have been coerced to have sex with someone else, you must get checked for STIs (sexually transmitted infections) even if you used protection. It is very important that you take responsibility for your own sexual health and ensure that you are aware of any STIs and gain the appropriate treatment and support if they have been passed on to you.

1 Recognise that you and your body are worth the effort of getting medical proof that you are STI-free. Do not depend on your partner to tell you the truth about their sexual infidelity or believe them if they say that it was "only once", or that they used protection.

2 Go on your own or with a supportive person to a sexual health (GUM) clinic, in the UK these are usually drop-in clinics.

3 It's not as scary as you think it might be. Clinics are there to do the testing and are used to seeing a wide variety of people at all ages and stages of life. They do not make judgements, but rather focus on your sexual health and ensuring you know your own health status and treatments available if you have an STI. The clinics are not only for those who have sex with multiple partners. It can be that you have an infection from one long-term partner who has been unfaithful and there is no shame in going. The medical staff see many people every day and will not judge.

More information on going to a clinic can be found at: *netdoctor.co.uk/healthy-living/sex-life/a26975/what-to-expect-sexual-health-clinic/*

> If you can, talk to God, He can take your anger, hurt and pain.

 TOP TIP It is important that you get the right treatment and support going forward, whatever you have been through. The first step is to seek out safe support. Take that first step.

Notes

Reference
1 We Need to Talk about Sex Addiction (Paula Hall, 2017). (Accessed on 03/11/18)
https://www.youtube.com/watch?time_continue=11&v=-Qf2e3XZ8Tw

....

Some websites and resources to have a look at:
The Life Centre in Chichester has a telephone helpline for survivors. Tel: 0808 802
0808/Text. 07717 989022 www.lifecentre.uk.com/

RAINN operates the US National Sexual Assault Hotline, accessible 24/7
by phone (800.656.HOPE) and online (https://online.rainn.org).

Rape Crisis England and Wales 0808 802 9999 www.rapecrisis.org.uk

The Laurel Centre for understanding sexual addiction and support for partners in the
UK, Holland & Dubai www.thelaurelcentre.co.uk/about-us

Partners of Sex Addicts Resource Centre www.posarc.com/

Beyond Support is a free, confidential UK wide phone/email callback service for
women who are or have been involved in selling sex www.beyondsupport.org.uk

Notes

By Esther Sweetman

CHAPTER 19

Infidelity and its Link to Domestic Abuse

A Challenge to Prevailing Attitudes
Minimising Infidelity

Historically, society has used language that has served to minimise infidelity and its consequences. 'His few indiscretions', 'she strayed', 'he made a mistake'. These terms lead one to conclude that infidelity is a small interpersonal issue with no collateral damage. The assumption that infidelity can be compartmentalised in such a way that the unfaithful spouse can still be a decent husband/wife is also widespread.

Technology Can Facilitate Infidelity

The rise of technology and universal access to the internet/smartphones has led to effortless engagement with sexting, chat lines, pornography, dating websites for the married and easy access to individuals working in prostitution. Therapeutic intervention for sex addiction has become a growing industry, whilst the call to personal responsibility and accountability is constantly diminishing.

Infidelity is Abuse

Reducing infidelity to sexual incompatibility or relationship issues and labelling ongoing extra-marital sexual relations as *sex addiction* - a sickness to be treated - ignores the fact that infidelity itself is abuse and ignores the role that infidelity plays in a larger pattern of abusive behaviour. Inherent in the act of infidelity is chronic lying, scheming, manipulation, blame-shifting and duplicity, which are all psychological patterns of abusive behaviour. In addition, the unfaithful spouse may be depleting the family bank account (financial abuse) to pay for gifts and dinners for affair partners or for pornography and paying people who work in prostitution.

Furthermore, the unfaithful spouse can be routinely and negligently choosing to risk their marriage partner's sexual health by potentially exposing them to sexually transmitted infections (physical abuse) with long term physical consequences, for example, HIV. This behaviour also knowingly takes away the faithful partner's right to make decisions regarding their sexual health, or actively practice safe sex.

This abuse of power (through secrecy) and control (through lies and manipulation) denies the faithful partner the ability to make their own informed choices. It also points to the unfaithful partner's sense of entitlement expressed through their complete disregard for their partner's wellbeing; blocking their partner's prerogative to leave a faithless marriage, and tricking faithful partners into participating in a happy family pretence - a sham, a lie. The unfaithful partner knowingly remains in the one-up position, while the faithful partner ignorantly remains subjugated.

> The unfaithful spouse can be routinely and negligently choosing to risk their marriage partner's sexual health.

The Reality of Infidelity
While the unfaithful partner may have a public reputation that is beyond reproach, the reality is that infidelity rarely happens in a vacuum. It is frequently associated with diminishing and devaluing a spouse (emotional and verbal abuse) which often occurs in the tension building phase of the cycle of abuse. The unfaithful partner might want an excuse to engage in extramarital sexual activity and so they may repeatedly provoke, pick fights or set up their spouse in such a way as to actively create conflict, purposefully fostering conditions that allow themselves to feel justified in their unfaithfulness. Years of living through this level of continuous stress can create physical and emotional ill-health on the part of the faithful spouse.

Abuse Thrives in Secrecy
Extramarital sexual behaviours can go on for years. The patterns of emotional, psychological, financial and physical abuse can also go on for years, resulting in the faithful partner struggling in a fog, feeling diminished and disrespected, without truly understanding what is going on. Abusers may feel entitled to a double life to fulfil their wants and needs. They feel that the fulfilment of their needs outweighs the importance of their partner's and/ or their children's well-being. In addition, it is common that the unfaithful partner will subtly encourage the isolation of their partner/family so that their behaviour is not identified or challenged by others. This isolation simultaneously removes potential support from the faithful partner.

Discovering Infidelity
When found out, the unfaithful partner may not take responsibility for their actions and may not feel that they

should be held accountable. The habitual mental justification required to continue being unfaithful has now become solidified. They may well shift blame and gather allies (friends, family, helping professional) to their side by subtly or overtly leaving the impression that their partner is unstable, hard to live with or has insurmountable failings. The aim is always to gain sympathy from others and capitalise on society's unchallenged acceptance that infidelity is mutually created by partners - in hopes that their allies will then overlook the abusive nature of their behaviour.

Rethinking the Issues

Infidelity is being normalised within society. The abusive behaviour involved is overlooked, the consequences minimised and unfaithful partners are rarely held to account or challenged to take responsibility.

The patterns of abuse involved with infidelity can have long-term effects on a faithful partner's sexual health, physical/mental health and emotional well being. The consequences of infidelity go way beyond the common, simplistic description of "hurt and betrayal". The road to recovery starts with acknowledging the abuse in the first place.

What next, if you find yourself in this situation?

1. Talk to someone you trust and who understands domestic abuse.
2. Find out about your local domestic abuse service provider and ask for advice, information and support.
3. Know that your partner's choices are his alone and are not related to anything you have or have not done. You are not responsible for his behaviour.
4. Get a sexual health check as soon as possible - you can find your nearest sexual health clinic online or speak to your GP.
5. Decide your next steps and the help and support you need.

 TOP TIP Challenge society's minimisation of the abusive nature of infidelity and its consequences.

Notes

By Susie Flashman-Jarvis

CHAPTER 20

Pornography and its link to Domestic Abuse

To understand the possible link between pornography and domestic abuse, it is important to look at the effects of pornography on the brain as well as on relationships.

The Effects on the Brain

Anything that we do - watching a good film, reading a good book or enjoying a delicious meal releases the feel-good chemical dopamine into the reward centre of the brain. This results in individuals seeking this feeling again and again. And because the brain has neuroplasticity, in other words, it can be re-hardwired, it means that what we look at and the habits we develop can have long-term positive and negative results.

Researchers have found that pornography affects the brain in similar ways to harmful substances like tobacco and drugs, making the brain release the same chemicals[1]. As with substance abuse, the porn watcher requires more and more of the porn 'drug' to get their 'high' and needs more and more extreme images to ensure the same level of sexual gratification. Images often increase in violence, scenarios become more dangerous, often involving young people and more people[2].

It compels the user or addict to ensure that their access to porn is achieved at any cost. But, as with any addiction, there are ways to get support. It is possible to quit porn and replace it with healthy habits[3]. It is a choice and requires that the user step out of denial and take responsibility for their own actions. The Naked Truth Project[4] runs an online recovery course for porn users.

The Effects on Relationships

People are wired for belonging and will often seek any way to connect. But in a world that has so many ways of connecting, we are facing increasing levels of isolation. Viewing pornography increases the viewer's sense of isolation and fuels self-seeking thinking around sex. It becomes a 'needs must' way of thinking and is all about meeting the individual's need.

As a therapist, I have often worked with couples on issues of communication, only to discover that the true problem is related to pornography use. I have often heard women say that they feel betrayed, as if their partner was having an affair, only to be faced with the blank faces of their partners.

Fight the New Drug (www.fightthenewdrug.org) is a research-based organisation that raises awareness of the harmful effects of pornography, based on science and facts. They outline, through an overview of research in the field, that those who regularly watch porn are often oblivious to the needs and views of their part-

ner. They refer to studies that show that even casual porn consumption can cause the porn user to feel less attracted to their partner. 'It makes porn users less satisfied with their partners' physical appearance, sexual performance, sexual curiosity, and affection'[5]. They also show that, over time, many porn users grow more callous toward women in general, less likely to value faithfulness and marriage, and more likely to develop distorted perceptions of sexuality[5]. They cite other researchers who have shown that porn users tend to be significantly less intimate with their partners, less committed in relationships, less satisfied with their romantic and sex lives, and more likely to cheat on their partners.[5]

> The media has already increased the pressure for women to look a certain way - slim and faultless.

The Effects on Sexual Intimacy

The media has already increased the pressure for women to look a certain way - slim and faultless. The women in pornography are often surgically enhanced, airbrushed or photoshopped - so how can a real-life woman compete with that?

The images on the screen are fictional and make the sexual acts look attractive and exciting. The participants look keen and eager, always ready for sex whatever the situation. Coercion into sex (rape) is normalised and thus becomes a legitimate and valid way to behave. With persistent viewing of pornographic images, the brain becomes almost immune to the levels of violence that are being watched. Images which at one time would have horrified the person watching, become normal viewing.

And porn keeps getting more extreme. "A competitive market means that pornographers are trying to outdo each other to come up with the most extreme images," explains Dr John Wood, a therapist who works with youth addicted to pornography. "This contest to push the boundaries means that straight intercourse is considered too boring. Images of brutal anal sex and women being humiliated and degraded by two or more men at any one time are the new norms[6]."

Fight the New Drug highlights Dr Michael Kimmel's findings that men's sexual fantasies have become heavily influenced by porn. This becomes problematic when partners don't want to act out the degrading or dangerous acts that porn depicts. As a result, individuals who consume pornography are more likely to go to prostitutes, often looking for a chance to live out what they've seen in porn. In one survey of former prostitutes, 80% said that customers had shown them images of porn to illustrate what they wanted to do[7].

The Gottman Institute, offers a research based approach to relationships and states that 'intimacy for couples is a source of connection and communication *between* two people. But when one person becomes accustomed to masturbating to porn, they are actually turning away from intimate interaction. Second, when watching pornography, the user is in total control of the sexual experience, in contrast to normal sex in which people are sharing control and intimacy with

"A competitive market means that pornographers are trying to outdo each other to come up with the most extreme images".

their partner. Pornography can also lead to a decrease in relationship trust and a higher likelihood of affairs outside the relationship[8].'

If more and more people are watching pornography, both men and women, what is the fall-out on relationships?

- Dr Jill Manning, a researcher in relationships, was quoted by Monica Marshall[9]: 'in the US 56 percent of divorce cases involve one party having an obsessive interest in pornographic websites.'

- Dr John Gottman (The Gottman Institute) also states: 'the research on marital intimacy in the US aligns with what divorce lawyers have been witnessing for at least the past fifteen years: Porn use destroys marital intimacy and significantly increases the chances that your marriage will end'.

The Effects on Young People

Pornography is now regarded as the main way that young people learn about sex. Many charities and schools are trying their best to provide a healthier way to think about sex through educational initiatives but the statistics are not encouraging.

- In the United States of America 92 billion pornographic videos watched, translates into "64 million visitors per day, or 44,000 [viewed] every minute. Collectively, that's 4.6 billion hours of porn watching stuffed into just one year." (Dines and Walker, 2017)[10]

- New research from security technology companies suggests that children under the age of 10 now account for 22% of under 18's online porn consumption while 10-14 year olds account for 36% of underage users[11].

- A study done by Middlesex University found that repeated viewing of online pornography may have a desensitising effect with young people feeling less negative over time and generally less anxious or disgusted by what they are seeing[12].

Men may end up objectifying women to such a degree when they use pornography that they believe the role of women is to satisfy their needs.

So, what is the link between domestic abuse and pornography?

Over the years I have worked with many women caught up in the cycle of domestic abuse. These women may have suffered repeated physical and sexual assault. They may have been isolated by their partner. They may have been undermined, psychologically abused, diminished and lost any sense of self-worth. As I have sat with couples who bring the remains of their relationship to me, the subject of sex invariably comes up, and the issue and effect of pornography.

I am aware that women also look at pornography but in the instances of couples that I have worked with, pornography use and addiction lies predominantly with men. There is nonetheless, a high degree of addiction of both men and women in the 18-30 age group.

The reasons cited as to why pornography is used, range from coping with stress, loneliness, tiredness, to relationship difficulties. One man is quoted as saying: '...before I knew it porn had become a powerful anaesthetic to treat any kind of anxiety, boredom and stress. It started to control my life...' extract from *The P Word Conference*[13].

Why do I believe that there is a link between pornography and domestic abuse?

Men may end up objectifying women to such a degree when they use pornography that they believe the role of women is to satisfy their needs. This delivers a fundamental change in how they regard women in reality. What they see in their face to face relationships cannot come up to scratch. The expectation is that women should be willing participants in any sexual act and scenario. Love and affection, respect and desire to please their partner gets lost in the urge for satisfaction at any cost[14].

Domestic abuse is about power and control, thus the man who wields power over his partner in an abusive manner, has his views consolidated when he watches pornography. What he views online reinforces his personal views and, in my opinion, solidifies them to such a degree that the fantasy world becomes part of his real-world view.

For porn users, even those who manage to avoid violent material, it's difficult not to be influenced. '*Study after study has* found that watching even non-violent porn is correlated with the consumer being more likely to use verbal coercion, drugs, and alcohol to coerce individuals into sex'. And 'There is clear evidence that porn makes many consumers more likely to support violence against women, to believe that women secretly enjoy being raped, and to actually be sexually aggressive in real life' [15].

Facts:

In Emily Rothman's (2015) article *Domestic Violence - What's Porn Got to do With It?*[16] written for Boston University's School of Public Health, she states that one area where research is becoming increasingly clear is the contribution of sexually explicit material to partnership abuse.

For porn users, even those who manage to avoid violent material, it's difficult not to be influenced.

- One study showed that long term exposure to violent sexually explicit material led to a 6 fold increase in self-reported sexually aggressive behaviours.
- Several studies showed women were expected by their partners to participate in or re-enact what they had viewed online, such as anal sex, even if it hurt them.
- Research analysing the content of pornography finds that the majority (88 percent) of mainstream internet pornography features slapping, gagging and spanking women.
- Approximately 43 percent of sexually explicit videos show women being submissive, while only 10 percent show men in that role.

Rothman concludes by stating that partnership behaviour, including abuse and sexual coercion, does not happen in a vacuum. What is becoming increasingly accepted by society in regards to sexually explicit material promoted by books, movies, music and videos influences how people treat one another and this in turn influences the ongoing development of these materials. She says it is equally important to note that a generation may be internalising sexual ideas and arousal cues from images of human pain and degradation.

A husband has no right to a woman's body against her will!

Women are often charged with the responsibility of getting a meal on the table, keeping house, dressing in a certain way or relieving their partners' stress. In this way sex can be reduced to simply meeting a man's needs, rather than engaging in a mutually loving experience. Ultimately, sex can become another way to diminish, overpower and suppress a woman. Pornography depicts sex where there is no need to show love and consideration.

Some women believe that rape is not possible in marriage as it is the right of the husband to demand sex. However, marital rape is a form of sexual assault under UK law, in contravention of the Sexual Offences Act 2003[17]. Rape is any forced act that is penetrative (that means using anything) and is against the woman's will.

- It does not mean you are abnormal if you do not wish to participate in anal sex
- You do not have to act out scenarios that are against your wishes
- You do not have to have sex with other people to satisfy him
- You are not responsible for his pornography use/addiction because he says sex with you is boring.

What now?

It is crucial that both women and men understand the facts. Pornography has been normalised over the past decade and this has resulted in both men and women becoming confused about its impact on society and on their relationship. Power and control will be played out in all areas of a relationship by an abuser, and this includes the sexual aspect of a relationship, so it is crucial that women are informed.

 TOP TIP Understand the facts regarding the influence of pornography in a user's life and its links to domestic abuse.

References

1 University of Cambridge:Research (2014). **Brain activity in sex addiction mirrors that of drug addiction.** www.cam.ac.uk/research/news/brain-activity-in-sex-addiction-mirrors-that-of-drug-addiction (accessed online 18 /10/18).

2 Fight the New Drug (2017). **How porn affects the brain like a drug.** fightthenewdrug.org/how-porn-affects-the-brain-like-a-drug/ (accessed online 18/10/17).

3 Fight the New Drug (2017). **Why consuming porn is an escalating behaviour.** fightthenewdrug.org/why-consuming-porn-is-an-escalating-behavior (accessed online 18/10/18).

4 The Naked Truth Project. thenakedtruthproject.com/354-2 (accessed online 18/10/18).

5 Fight the New Drug (2017). **How porn hurts a consumers partner.** (accessed online 18/10/18). fightthenewdrug.org/how-porn-hurts-a-consumers-partner/

6 Woods, J. (2012). **Jamie is 13 and hasn't even kissed a girl. But he's now on the Sex Offender Register after online porn warped his mind...** www.dailymail.co.uk/news/article-2135203/Jamie-13-kissed-girl-But-hes-Sex-Offender-Register-online-porn-warped-mind-.html (accessed online 18/10/18).

7 Fight the New Drug (2017). **How porn warps ideas about sex.** fightthenewdrug.org/how-porn-warps-ideas-about-sex/ (accessed 18/10/18).

8 Gottman, J&J (2016). **An open letter on porn.** www.gottman.com/blog/an-open-letter-on-porn/ (accessed 18/10/18).

9 Marshall, M.G. (2017). - **Divorce Lawyers Say this is Why Marriages are Falling Apart: It is more than just 'irreconcilable differences'** verilymag.com/2017/07/causes-of-divorce-effects-of-watching-pornography (accessed 18/10/18).

10 Dines and Walker (2017) **You'd be Surprised to Hear what Porn is Doing to Sex.** verilymag.com/2017/07/porn-is-ruining-sex-say-recovering-sex-addicts (accessed 18/10/18).

11 Fight the New Drug (2018). One in 10 visitors to hardcore porn sites is under 10 years old, study shows. fightthenewdrug.org/data-says-one-in-10-visitors-to-porn-sites-are-under-10-years-old/ (accessed on 18/10/18).

12 NSPCC (2018). *I wasn't sure it was normal to watch it.* learning.nspcc.org.uk/research-resources/2016/i-wasn-t-sure-it-was-normal-to-watch-it/ (accessed 18/10/18).

13 The Naked Truth Project thenakedtruthproject.com

14 Fight the New Drug. (2017). **How porn kills love.** fightthenewdrug.org/how-porn-kills-love/ (accessed 18/10/18).

15 Fight the New Drug (2017). *How consuming porn can lead to violence.* fightthenewdrug.org/how-consuming-porn-can-lead-to-violence/ (accessed 18/10/18).

16 Rothman, Emily (2015) *Domestic Violence - What's Porn Got to do With It?* www.bu.edu/sph/2015/10/20/viewpoint-domestic-violence-whats-porn-got-to-do-with-it/ (accessed 18/10/18).

17 Sexual Offences Act 2003. (accessed 30/1018). www.legislation.gov.uk/ukpga/2003/42/contents

Notes

By Ally Kern

CHAPTER 21

Healing Practices

Recovering from domestic abuse is a challenging journey and it can feel overwhelming at times. The good news is that healing and transformation is possible! Yes, it takes commitment and hard work, but we know first hand that with consistent small steps, even a few minutes a day can make a big difference. This chapter is full of amazing resources that have been demonstrated to facilitate internal stability, peace and well-being. I encourage you to start by choosing 1-2 exercises to incorporate into your daily routine to begin with. Just 5 minutes a day will empower you to regain control of your life and help you build a new future where you can flourish.

. . . .

PRAYER
Breath Prayers

Introduction

What could be more simple than breathing, right? In the business of everyday life, however, it is essential to carve out some time to slow down and simply be present to ourselves. When we regularly take time to slow down our breathing, we are actually doing something amazing for our mind, body and soul! By following the technique below, you are intentionally causing your body to relax and nurture peace to flow through your entire being.

Breath prayers have a long history in the spiritual formation of the Christian church. The Desert Fathers—monastic Christians in Egypt in the third and fourth centuries—often prayed the prayer many know as the "Kyrie Eleison" (Greek for *"Lord, have mercy"*). Also called the "Jesus Prayer," it is rooted in Psalm 123:3, Luke 18:13, and Luke 18:38.

You choose a brief phrase that can be repeated in one breath. As we breathe, we're simply using our bodies to engage our mind and heart with God's Word that restores our souls. This simple practice can be very helpful in calming our fears and anxieties and cultivating peace within, and only takes just a minute or two.

Activity

A Breath Prayer rhythm is simple: Breathe in slow and deep as you whisper or think on God's compassion or a Bible phrase... Hold your breath... Then exhale. It's that easy.

Follow these simple steps:

1. Ideally, find a place where you can be alone and quiet for a few minutes. Sit comfortably and let your body relax.
2. Choose a phrase to focus on as you breathe in. This could be, "God loves me", "God, I belong to you," or whatever is meaningful to you in the moment.
3. Breathe in *slowly* and *steadily* through your nose for a count of 4. Imagine yourself breathing in God's love and compassion for you as you pray your chosen phrase.
4. Pause for a few seconds.
5. Exhale *slowly* and *steadily* for a count of 4. Try to breathe out with a sigh. Imagine you are releasing your stress, anxiety, fear, or anything holding you back.
6. Repeat for a few minutes until you notice a change in how your body feels.

7. If you get distracted, or your mind wanders, just bring your attention back to how it feels to breathe in and out. Allow yourself to rest in God's compassionate love for you.

Mindfulness Prayers

Introduction

Our minds can be full of racing thoughts and we can easily get caught up in worry, insecurity, doubt, despair and even self-harm. Through mindfulness prayers we can draw our attention away from such painful thoughts towards peace and health. Mindfulness is our universal human capacity for awareness and attention. Basically, it means being intentional about what we're thinking about. Biblical scholars recognize the gospel is an embodied gospel, and mindfulness is the embodied awareness that enables us to enter into God's freedom within our emotional and spiritual self. Just as Jesus calls us to be mindful of today (Matt. 6), we can practice being present and purposeful about what we are thinking. You'll find the benefits can range from reduced stress, enhanced happiness, a calm mind, reduced physical pain, minimised anxiety and more!

Activity

1. Choose a place where you can be alone and quiet for a few minutes. Sit comfortably and let your body relax.
2. Let your awareness find your breath. Completely immerse yourself in the experience of breathing.
3. As you breathe out with a sigh, extend the out breath just a little bit longer.
4. Try not to get caught up in any thoughts, but if you do, just remind

yourself that you can go back to a thought afterwards. Refocus on breathing in and out slowly.

5. Notice what you're feeling, without judgement, without engaging, just notice. Notice if the feeling shows up anywhere in particular in your body.

6. *Imagine a wave of God's loving kindness flowing through your body, starting with your toes and moving up to your head. Bring all your awareness to this feeling.*

7. *Focus on the felt sense of Jesus' compassion and love* physically permeating your body. As vividly as you can, receive this gift from God, feeling it flow through you fully for a few minutes.

8. *Slowly*, at your own pace, begin to bring your awareness back to your breathing, paying attention to how you're feeling as you shift back to the room.

9. *Reflect* back to Jesus a prayer offering whatever insights you gained during this time.

Listening Prayer

Introduction

Praying is not only talking to God, it is also listening to God. God longs to speak with us. 1 Corinthians 2:6 tells us that as Christ followers, we have the mind of Christ. Similarly, John 10 reminds us that God's children hear God's voice. This means that our thoughts—when directed by the Holy Spirit—can become a vehicle in prayer to hear God's truth (John 16: 12-15). We need to take time regularly to hear God's voice—his promises, his

> **Through mindfulness prayers we can draw our attention away from such painful thoughts towards peace and health.**

loving presence, comfort and encouragement. The good news is that we can learn to recognise God's voice by regularly listening, as it will confirm the words of Scripture—especially Jesus' words, and it will bear fruit in your life, such as peace, joy, faith, comfort and love within. Jesus' voice will not be one of fear, anxiety, or shame. Rather, as 1 Corinthians 14:3 affirms, God's voice strengthens, comforts, and encourages us.

This spiritual practice of learning to hear God's voice through the presence of the Holy Spirit within is based on Jesus' regular practice of listening to the Father (John 8:28; 12:49). True spiritual listening is an act of suspending judgement, advice-giving, listening for the purpose of giving an answer, or imposing one's own experience on another, in the realisation that Jesus is the ultimate healer and solution to one's soul pain, not oneself.

Activity

How do you listen to an all-powerful but invisible God? The Bible reveals over and over how God interacts with people in a variety of ways. Our God is endlessly creative in how he communicates with us! We just need to make the time to listen.

1. Find a place where you can have 5-15 minutes to be quiet. This could be out in nature, taking a walk in a park, sitting in your favourite chair. It might be helpful to have your journal and a pen with you to write down what God shares with you.

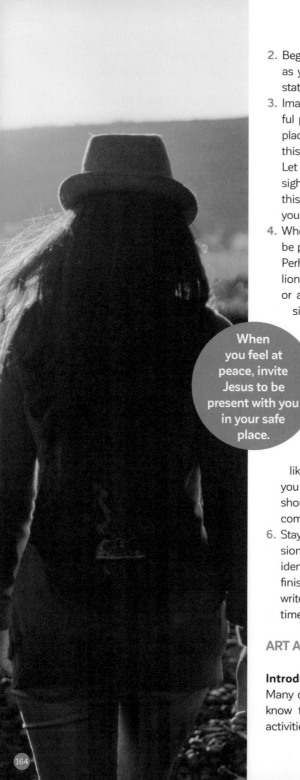

2. Begin with a few slow, deep breaths as you settle your body into a relaxed state.

3. Imagine in your mind a safe, peaceful place. It can be a real or imagined place, but just allow yourself to picture this safe place as vividly as you can. Let your body be fully present to the sights, sounds, smells and textures of this place. Breathe in deeply the peace you feel here!

4. When you feel at peace, invite Jesus to be present with you in your safe place. Perhaps Jesus appears to you as the lion from Narnia—Aslan, or a butterfly, or a gentle carpenter, or maybe even simply a colour or sensation of compassion. Allow your God-given creativity to connect with Jesus as you feel safe to.

> When you feel at peace, invite Jesus to be present with you in your safe place.

5. When you feel at peace with Jesus' presence with you in your safe place, try to look at Jesus and ask him a question. Perhaps you could begin with, "Jesus, what do you like about me?" Whatever questions you ask, remember that Jesus' voice should strengthen, encourage and comfort you.

6. Stay for a few minutes in this compassionate presence as Jesus affirms your identity as his beloved daughter. Then finish by taking a couple of minutes to write or draw your reflections on your time of listening prayer.

ART AS HEALING

Introduction

Many of our wounds are invisible, yet we know their pain profoundly. Arts-based activities enable us to have the freedom to express our wounds through painting, drawing, creating a song, writing, or other creative means. Here we can safely 'speak' out our suffering through putting images to our invisible wounds.

Journalling

Choose a journal or bind together some paper for your own, private journal. Decorate the cover of your journals with markers, pens, stickers, coloured paper, etc.

Activity

Take about three minutes for each idea, allowing yourself to be creative in how you express yourself. You could try different ways to communicate your thoughts and feelings, such as using colours, symbols, or images, as well as words. Remember that you don't have to share your journal with anyone unless you choose to do so.

- Decide what colour each feeling might be: happy, sad, angry, calm, lonely etc. Use one or more of the colours to create a scribble drawing showing how you feel right now.
- What can you draw that might show something about yourself?
- Draw or write about a favourite part of your day. What did it look like? Sound like? Smell like? Taste like? Feel like?
- Without stopping, write for 3 minutes. The idea is to write without thinking critically about what you're writing. Complete the sentences, writing for 1 minute on as many of these topics as you would like: I like...I want...I need...I feel...I am...

After you have drawn or written, take a few minutes to reflect on how you felt about the activity, and anything you learned about yourself while journaling with art.

Collage

Collages are an age-old way to find words or pictures that mean something to you in that moment, combine them together, and see what emerges. You may be surprised to see what comes to the surface that you didn't know was there.

Activity

1. Gather together your supplies, such as construction paper, plain paper, paper bags, tissue paper, magazines, newspapers, marbled paper, handmade paper, foil, cotton, fabric, buttons, glue, tape, paint, crayons, pens, etc. Try finding mixed materials of different sizes, shapes, textures, look and so on.

2. Fold, cut or tear the paper into different shapes. You can use scissors or a craft knife to make different shapes. Alternatively, you can make rough tears on the ends of the paper pieces for more texture or a less controlled look. Cut out a whole picture, an identifiable part, or just enough to evoke texture, colour, or feeling. To make a word, cut out letters from sources which use different fonts.

3. You can develop a theme or just start drawing, painting and attaching various bits of paper or other materials to your paper. You could collage your values, your gratitude, your suffering or grief, meaningful words or feelings, or a self-portrait, or you can be spontaneous and see what emerges! Allow yourself to be where you're at and to explore new possibilities of art, understanding and visual expression wherever you're at in the moment.

4. Take a moment when you're finished—or maybe your artwork is still in progress—and encourage yourself for your bravery to be creative and to be yourself!

Safe Place Stone

Introduction
Sometimes it helps to remind ourselves that we are no longer in crisis. The more we focus our attention on our present safety, the easier it is to truly embrace and feel the peace and health of our journey in recovery and transformation. By imagining a 'safe place' in our mind and then holding on to that through a physical item—such as a stone—we can grab hold of peace and live deeper into it.

Activity
1. Brainstorm about all the things you love to do and places you love to go. Write them down.
2. Grab some supplies (Sharpies, clear gemstones with a flat bottom and curved top, tacky glue, paper and scissors).
3. Cut out a circle in the shape of your selected stone.
4. Go back to your list of things you love to do and places you love to go. Are any of these safe places for you?
5. If you could imagine a safe place (real or made up), what would it look like? Smell like? Feel like?
6. Draw that image on your circle. Take your time and then let the ink dry.
7. Put a pea sized dab of glue right on top of your picture.
8. Place the flat end of the stone on top of your picture.

Enjoy your finished product! And ponder... what will you do with your touchstone? Will you put it by your bed, place it in the bathroom, carry it in your pocket? The possibilities are endless!

THE RESILIENT BODY

Introduction
Our bodies have been through a lot and may still be a source of pain today. As part of our journey of healing from trauma, it's important that we nourish a positive connection with our body, and also release the often long-held tension it has stored. Through the following practices, we can learn to accept and embrace ourselves and through gentle and compassionate attention to our bodies, reclaim them as our own.

Body Scan
Sometimes it can be too difficult to put words to our experiences, emotions and thoughts. Body scan meditation allows you the opportunity to connect with yourself in the present moment through awareness of your body—to stop and listen to what your body is communicating to you. God made us as physical beings, not just mental and emotional beings. We can assume that this was intentional—that there is value in paying attention to this part of God's creation that is the body. Your body, along with the rest of you, reflects God's image (Gen. 1:27) and is a "temple of the Holy Spirit" (1 Cor. 6:19). God lives within you. If you want to experience God, experiencing your body is an excellent place to begin.

The body scan has been shown to be a powerful tool in improving health and facilitating relaxation, both physical and mental. It also enhances your ability to focus your attention at will. You may find this exercise to be relaxing, frustrating, confusing, or boring—whatever your experience, you can congratulate yourself on taking this step into a deeper and richer life. The benefits of mindfulness meditation will come with practice over time.

Activity

1. Let your awareness find your breath. In a place in your torso that feels comfortable, bring your attention. Could be your heart, or deep down in your belly. Wherever you want to focus on your breath. Immerse yourself in the experience of breathing. If you can extend the out breath just a little bit longer than the in breath, it will help calm and centre you.

2. From a witnessing or observing point of view, notice what your thoughts and feelings are. Simply observe from a little distance so they don't have a hold on you. If you want, you can repeat the word 'release' on the out breath and physically feel the sensation of release.

3. Now imagine a wave of relaxation starting at your toes and slowly moving up through your feet, your ankles, deep into your legs, hips, and torso, back and chest. Just feel the sensation of release. Imagine this wave of relaxation slowly making its way up through your shoulder blades. You can feel a profound wave of release as this wave passes through. Then simultaneously down each arm. Then very slowly this wave of relaxation is making its way up

the back of the neck and when it gets to the base of your skull it's like a cap unfolding, beginning to encircle and engulf the skull. As it begins to encircle your skull, you can feel yourself just letting go of all the tension and stress you carry in your head.

4. As you move, slowly scanning your body, remember to immerse yourself in the experience of breathing in God's compassion. As deeply as you can, imagine your entire body, mind and soul overflowing with God's loving kindness and calming presence.

> Sometimes just moving our body and getting our muscles engaged can help us feel better.

Walking Exercise

Sometimes just moving our body and getting our muscles engaged can help us feel better, and move us towards healing and well-being.

There is all sorts of research demonstrating that simply walking 30-minutes a day has enormous emotional and physical benefits. There is tremendous richness of experience to become aware of as you walk, cycle, play at a park or playground, or relax your body through yoga. By intentionally focusing on Christ's compassionate presence with us in the midst of any of these physical activities, we can participate in experiential worship that deepens our connection to Christ through his Word, worship and wellness.

Activity

The body loves movement, and will reward us with pleasure if we pay attention to how it feels! So much of the time we are caught up in our mental worlds, but taking 15-30 minutes a day to pay attention to our body as we do physical exercise can help us enjoy simply being alive.

1. Before you begin your exercise of choice, take a minute or two to simply become aware of your body while standing still. Take some deep breaths, noticing how your body feels as you are standing, and becoming aware of all the sensations going on in your body. You might also imagine Jesus with you and feel his compassion flowing through your body.

2. As you gently begin exercising, try and keep your attention on the loving presence of Christ, and the movement of your body. Notice the sensations of your body—including places of tension—breathing slowly in and out as you relax your muscles.

3. Throughout your time of exercise, be patient and kind to yourself, allowing yourself to move as feels best for you and your body. When you notice your thoughts moving away from Christ and your body, gently bring your awareness back to compassion and the movement of your body.

4. When you have finished, take a moment to reflect how you felt during this time. Consider how you might incorporate different forms of exercise into your daily routine—even if it's just 10 minutes!

TOP TIP Choose the healing practice that suits your personality and interests.

Mandy Marshall Co-Founder and Co-Director of Restored

CHAPTER 22

What Next? Rebuilding your life after abuse

Well done! You have survived and decided to move on. That is the first, courageous step, taking you into the rest of your life. You may not feel like you deserve a 'well done' as society often views relationship breakdown as a failure. However, it's important to be clear you are not responsible for the abuse inflicted on you. The person choosing to abuse you is responsible for the break in your relationship, not you. You have moved on for your own self-preservation and to enjoy, yes enjoy, life in all its fullness.

God Loves You

It is really important to remember that God's love for you has not changed. It is unconditional. It always was and always will be. We do not earn God's love. He loves you enough to send Jesus to model a life of love - how to treat other people in relationships and how to expect to be treated. Think about the woman who was bleeding. She had been bleeding for twelve years and is desperate for healing. She reaches out and touches Jesus and immediately she is healed. Jesus stops and asks who has touched him, and the woman comes trembling to Jesus. Jesus speaks life to her and heals her further when he says 'Daughter, your faith has healed you, go in peace' (Luke:8:48). Jesus acknowledges the woman's faith, her need to be healed, and heals her. He also restores her amongst the community by declaring in front of the crowd that she is now healed. It means she can also worship at the temple again. Jesus longs for us to come to him for love and healing. He won't force or coerce us. He waits patiently for us to ask. And when we do ask, he brings love and healing.

Self-Audit

Conducting our own self audit regarding the lies, misinformation and sometimes our own misunderstanding of what we have been told or believed over the years is a good place to start. Get a notebook and split a page into two columns. Down the first column, write all the lies, misinformation and misunderstandings you have been told, or absorbed about yourself during the abuse you have suffered. List the lot. It might be hard to start but once you do it may well be a long list. In the next column write the truth about the situation. So, for example, you may believe that you are a failure. In the next column list all the things you have achieved in leaving the abuser, eg I survived, I have new accommodation, I have supportive friends and family, I have found a new school for the children, I'm now managing my own budget, I'm wearing clothes that I choose to wear. Write down anything positive that counters the lies. It is only once we see our list of

> It is only once we see our list of strengths, achievements and successes that we can begin to counter the untruths spoken over us and begin the mental rebuild of our lives.

strengths, achievements and successes that we can begin to counter the untruths spoken over us and begin the mental rebuild of our lives.

Dream Diary

Being with an abuser often means the focus of our thoughts, actions and life centred around someone else and their demands. Now that you are away from them you can start to focus on yourself (and your children if you have them) more than before. Give yourself the opportunity and space to let go of old dreams and consider new and better dreams. You may have been so focussed on the abuser that you have not had time to think about yourself, what you would like, what you want to do or even allowed yourself to dare to dream. 'I don't know what I want!' and 'I gave up dreaming a long time ago' or even my dream of a 'happy intact family has been destroyed' may be some of the first thoughts that come rushing to your mind. Right now all of those thoughts may well feel true, but like most things in life, it's about training or re-training our minds to think differently.

First, we do have to give ourselves the permission to think like that. Healing is a process and we may well need to talk through some of our losses with someone. However, a practical exercise that can help us through this stage is to write a list of new dreams. You may stare at a blank page for a long time at the beginning, but give yourself five minutes each day to dream.

Think back to what you wanted to do all those years ago; what would you like to do now? What desire have you long held that you have repressed, that can now rise to the surface again? It may be as simple as 'I've always wanted to see Blackpool Illuminations', or something more challenging like 'I want to train to be a paramedic'. And families come in many wonderful packages - they don't all have to look the same. What new dreams can you form for your family - new traditions and new fun? Again write them down. Don't dismiss them. Some of the items on the list will be easier, quicker and cheaper to achieve than others but keep them on the list as your Dream Diary. Once we start to give ourselves permission to dream again, you will be surprised at what new and exciting opportunities pop into your head during those five minutes each day.

New Life, New Friends

One of the many consequences of domestic abuse is that some of our friends, family and church community are supportive, others simply don't understand and others may side with your ex-partner. The new situation will mean some friends will support you and others will not, or will slowly fall away. And you may have had to find a new, more supportive church community. Don't despair over these changes, it is an opportunity to make and build new friendships, when you feel ready and able to do so. It will be your choice to decide what to tell new people about your circumstances. You may want a fresh start where few know about your past, or you may want a friendly shoulder of support locally.

Is there a local church that you feel safe and able to join? They don't need to know your background unless you feel it is a safe space to disclose what you have been through. Finding a welcoming church is a place to start to rebuild your faith that may have been impacted by what you have gone through. It will take time.

Do you play a sport? Can you join a local club? If you run, or walk, Park Run (www. parkrun.org.uk) is a free event that takes place at 9am on Saturday mornings around the UK. It is a great place to meet new people, stay fit and healthy, (which is also good for mental health) and has the added benefit that children can come along too. If sport is not your thing, there are other local groups you could join to meet new people. Meet Up (www.meetup.com) is one place to find other like-minded individuals with similar interests. Is there a hobby that you have always liked that you have not been able to do, that you could pick up again? Have you always wanted to go sky-diving? Great, loads of charities offer this as a fundraising event. You could do it for free and raise funds for a vital cause too. Double the fun. You could fundraise for Restored and raise vital funds for our work too. (Please see *Fundraising Opportunities to support Restored* at the end of the Handbook.)

Friends Audit

Sounds horrible, doesn't it? We don't do that as Christians, surely not. We do, however, need to focus on what we need right now to rebuild our lives step by step. The reality is that some of your friends

Some friends will support you and others will not or will slowly fall away.

will simply not understand the trauma you have survived and may not be understanding or sympathetic. They may have expectations of you that are completely unrealistic. They may side with your abuser and expect you to remain friends with your abuser as well. As a result, you may choose to let these friends go as you move into this next phase of your life. It is OK to let these friends go. You have a choice. You need people in your life that will build you up, support and encourage you. We don't often think of letting go of friends, but it does naturally happen anyway as our life shifts through different stages.

It can be a little different in the age of social media but you can 'hide' friends if you are not quite able to 'unfriend' them yet. Our Christian culture subtly implies that we should get on with everyone, but it simply isn't true. God created diversity for a reason. Some people will like us and others won't, and that is just fine. It's the diversity of life. We can use a lot of energy trying to get along with people who we don't like under the compulsion that we think that's what God wants. We are called to love, and need to treat every individual as made in the image of God, with dignity and respect, but we don't have to be friends with them. Be kind to yourself. Which friends do you need in your life and which ones are not serving you well and can be let go?

New Home

Moving home is a huge change in your life (please refer to chapter 3: *Accommodation*). It's one of the top five stress factors in life, along with new job, death, illness and divorce/marriage. You've probably done at least two of them by this point so no wonder you may feel a bit stressed. Anyone would. You may not have had much choice as to where you have moved to in order to keep yourself and your children safe. Being in a new home gives you the opportunity to decorate it and have it how you want. Always wanted lime green paint on the walls? Do it! (If you are in rental accommodation please make sure you agree this with your landlord/lady first...) This is your house and home now, it's time to make it your own place. Always wanted a certain picture on the wall? Do it. Give yourself permission to do the things at home that you've wanted to do, that you may have been prevented from doing in the past. Sometimes we just need to give ourselves permission to do it. If you need someone else to give you permission, then I give you permission! Do all you can to make this new place a home.

Do all you can to make this new place a home.

New Vocation or Volunteering

Part of moving on may be about finding a new job and vocation (please refer to chapters 12 and 13 *Career Planning and Return to Work*). The first job you take may be more about survival than a dream job and that is OK. Your life has changed significantly and you need time to get to where you want to be. As you feel able, you may want to start searching for volunteer opportunities (if you have the capacity and time, appreciating that some of you will have young children).

Volunteering can get you a step on the next rung on the ladder of the job you want. For example, volunteering at a Christian event not only supports the charity who need volunteers, but it's an opportunity to meet new people, often gain some Christian teaching and it's free. It expands your network of contacts and gives you confidence, perhaps in areas that you didn't expect. Volunteering gives you a sense of self-worth alongside providing vital support where it is needed.

Dating Again

'Never again!' may be your first reaction to that heading. And, yes, dating may be in the distance for you as you heal, recover and restore your own sense of self-worth and value. All the internal work we need to do before venturing out onto the dating scene again is incredibly important and needs to be done - this may take some time, years even.

Gaining an understanding of what you have been through, ie domestic abuse, and knowing the signs and indicators of abuse are all necessary so that we are equipped to spot the signs in future. The Freedom Programme (freedomprogramme.co.uk) offers a good course on the different types of abuse, how the different types manifest themselves, and the values and beliefs that underpin the abuse (it's a secular course and there are lots of swear words used, so be warned if you would find that hard). However, it's an incredibly helpful course to understand what you have been through and enables you to safely process with people who understand. You can do it online too but it is better in groups if you can find one locally.

Now that you have information on what an abuser looks like, you can also know what a good man looks like too.

Now that you have information on what an abuser looks like, you can also know what a good man looks like too. The Freedom Programme describes this man as 'Not a saint you are seeing, just a decent human being', as often the characteristics of a decent bloke are so far removed from our own experiences that we think they must be an angel rather than human! Characteristics of a decent bloke include being kind and considerate, listening to your hopes and dreams, being thoughtful, encouraging and supportive, providing a shoulder to cry on, treating you as an equal, acknowledging when they are wrong and apologising, having a sense of humour and being cheerful, and taking responsibility for themselves. As I write this list, I can almost hear some of you dismissing it - no person looks like this. However, these are the qualities that we should be looking for in any new relationship. No-one is perfect, however we need to protect ourselves and ensure that the next person we date or form a relationship with, will enhance our life and not diminish it. (Please refer to chapter 17: Boundaries and Healthy Relationships.)

Online Dating

Dating may have moved on since you were last single. It can feel like a minefield with apps such as Tinder, Guardian Soulmates, Elite Singles, Plenty of Fish and Christian Connections to name a few. There are many to choose from and it is worth doing some research on which one feels right for you. Christian Connections, Christian Café and Fusion 101 are designed for the Christian community. However, we do not promote any particular dating site - do your own thorough checks before joining any site - some sites allow you to look around before joining.

Consider carefully what you may put on your profile. Ask a trusted friend to read over your profile information and give you honest feedback on it. You could also ask them to write it for you, for you to look over, as they may be able to bring out your best qualities. The words you use on some dating sites can also have hidden meaning. The word 'fun' can be one of those seemingly innocuous words that on some sites is code for looking for sex. Do check what you write is what you are wanting to communicate to others. **Do keep yourself safe online**. Don't be naive, some people are not honest about how they present themselves and we need to be wise and cautious about who we connect with online. This is especially true if your abuser is known for stalking and harassing you.

Keep yourself safe online.

The Date

You've done it, you've taken the steps to get online, connect with people, research their background and chat in advance with them online and then on a phone call to see if you connect. Now you are actually going on a date. But hang on, that dress you wore in 1995/2005/2015 may not fit, or be right for the occasion. Now is the time to treat yourself and update your wardrobe for the date. Depending on your budget, you can choose the high street shops or look in the charity shops that have some great bargains on some fabulous clothes and outfits. You do not need to spend a small fortune here if you can't afford to do so.

Take a friend shopping with you who will be honest about what you are choosing, and get the right outfit for the date. If you have arranged to meet up in a pub then jeans, boots and a decent top will suffice. If your date is in a restaurant, then you may want to opt for a dress or smart trousers and top. Pick the outfit that brings out the best in you, makes you feel good and you can relax and enjoy yourself on the date without worrying about a 'wardrobe malfunction'. If you want to wear makeup, you may want to treat yourself to some new products. Again there is a range available. If you don't want to wear any, then don't. This is the new you and the new you can make the choices and decisions about what you want. The same with jewellery. Choose if you want to wear it or not.

The key element on a date is to keep yourself safe at all times. Always meet in a public setting and tell a friend where you are meeting the person, what time, what time you are expecting to be home and agree to let them know you are home safe. This is really important to do. It will put you at ease and also gives your friends a chance to encourage you and support you, as well as ensure you are indeed safe. Have a chat with your friend the next day and tell them about it. It is helpful to talk it through as going on a date is a huge step forward in moving on. Well done!

Not the end, just the beginning

Yay, go you! You've started your new life, new self and made a new start. Congratulate yourself. That's not a very British thing to do, is it? Celebrate our own achievements? Sometimes our culture has to change. We need to be our own cheerleaders. Celebrate the small positive steps we have made to move onto the next one. Think of the London Marathon. Most runners have their name on their t-shirt as they run. There is a 26.2 mile cheer zone along the London Marathon route with strangers calling out names to encourage the runners. The supporters don't know every runner but if they see a name on a shirt often shouts of 'Come on Sally you can do it' can be heard, or 'Great job Clare, keep going'. Each morning when you get up God is cheering you on. God is your biggest cheerleader, because She/He is. As you wake up, think of God shouting your name and encouraging you on as you enter another day. We at Restored will be cheering you on too. We want you to know that the love of God restores, that there is life in all its fullness waiting for you. Go and grab life by both hands. We are cheering you on!

TOP TIP — God loves you and accepts you just the way you are. Be kind to yourself and keep yourself safe.

Notes

PART 4

THEOLOGICAL ISSUES RELATING TO DOMESTIC ABUSE

By Ally Kern

CHAPTER 23

What does the Bible really say about Domestic Abuse?

A Biblical Response to Domestic Abuse

You may have heard the phrase, 'God is love,' and wondered what that means in the context of domestic abuse. If you've even quickly skimmed through the Bible (especially the Old Testament), you've seen many stories of violence - from rape, to slavery, and war. The Bible recognizes that violence and abuse exist in society. While Scripture may have been used to keep us quiet about our experiences of abuse, to urge us to stay with an abusive partner, and even to justify the abuse, the Bible is clear that God opposes those who oppress, marginalize and abuse others.

But Jesus doesn't talk directly about abuse...

The life of Jesus is the biblical model for understanding God, and also a key way for us to identify how God responds to violence and abuse. Jesus' ministry is about exposing injustice and advocat-ing for the marginalised, oppressed and abused. He is particularly concerned about women and children, who are often considered less important in society, and made vulnerable by oppression and abuse. Jesus reminds us that the vulner-able are violated by the denial of justice, revealing God's heart for compassion, healing, and restoration to a full and equal life (Luke 11:46, 17:2, 18:1-8, John 8:2-11). This is why Jesus stops the stoning of the woman under suspicion of adultery (John 8:2-11), heals the bleeding woman (Luke 8:43-48), and speaks to the woman at the well who's had five husbands (John 4:4-42)—not because they have done something wrong, but because the men in their community had acted unjustly towards the women.

It may seem obvious that the person who abuses is the sinner but some Christians have attempted to justify or excuse abuse using Scripture.

This is what gets Jesus so angry that he flips the tables in the temple: it is the misuse and abuse of power and control by the religious leaders that perpetuates oppression and abuse against the vulnerable (Matt. 21:12). As men had the power and privilege in both family and society in biblical times—and still do today in most situations—Jesus addresses the marginalisation and abuse of these women by the men who should have protected and provided for them so they could flourish. By speaking to these, and other women in Scripture, Jesus brings them back into a position of status in society.

Who is sinning: the person who abuses, or the victim who wants to leave?

It may seem obvious that the person who abuses is the sinner but some Christians have attempted to justify or excuse abuse, using Scripture to back them up. However, this goes against the very nature of God, who is love. The Bible views all forms of domestic violence as sin (Malachi 2:16-17; Psalm 11:5; Colossians 3:19),

including verbal abuse (Prov. 12:18; Prov. 18:21; Matt.5:22; Colossians 3:8), and exhorts us to protect ourselves from violent people (Proverbs 27:12; Prov. 11:9). Even in troubled relationships where one is provoked, the Bible speaks out against responding with violence (Ephesians 4:26; Luke 6:45). Furthermore, God's heart is to deliver the abused (Psalms 5, 7, 10, 140; Acts 14:5-6). *Any form of abuse,* then, is unacceptable behaviour which directly defies God's calling for Christ-followers to relate to each other in love. The person who abuses is sinning, the victim who wants to leave is not in sin. While not everyone has the ability to leave an abusive partner, it is not wrong to attempt to do so if possible, for the Bible encourages victims to seek safety (Proverbs 22:3 and 27:12; 1 Samuel 20; Luke 4:28-29; Acts 9:23-25; Matthew 18:15-17).

God acts on behalf of the abused

We can see throughout the Bible that God is not passive about violence committed against women. God acts decisively and compassionately through Jesus to call all people to love mercy, act justly, and nurture healing and justice for everyone—most especially when power is used to harm others. The God of the Bible, then, is one who honestly tells the story of women who are abused—not to justify violence, but to tell the truth: that when men abuse women, God sees it and God's heart breaks for the abused. God acts clearly through the life and death of Jesus to take an ultimate stance against all forms of violence, oppression, marginalisation and abuse, declaring that 'God is love' and God's love will not stand passively or silently when women are abused (1 John 4:8).

TOP TIP The person who is abusing is sinning, the victim who wants to leave is not in sin.

Notes

By Ally Kern

CHAPTER 24

Is Domestic Abuse a Biblical Form of Suffering?

Doesn't Scripture say that I should suffer like Jesus—even unto death?

Throughout the life and ministry of Jesus we see that he talks lovingly with women who are mistreated and abused, (John 4:1-42; Matt. 9:20-22; Luke 7:11-15; Luke 13:10-17), disciples and ministers to women (Matt. 12:46-50; Matt. 27:55-56; Mark 1:30-31; Luke 8:1-3; Luke 10:38-42; John 20:11-18), and encourages their leadership in ministry and in the home (John 2:1-11; Acts 1:14). Jesus demonstrates that he sees women as equals who must be treated as valuable, with respect and with authority over their own lives. Yet often the role of suffering, as depicted in Jesus' death on the cross, is used to call women to stay in abusive marriages. Some clergy counsel women to stay with male partners who abuse them under the guise that their suffering is 'their cross to bear', and they must stay married for 'better or worse'.

You may have heard someone say that their pain is part of God's plan to humble them or teach them to be more Christ-like. After all, didn't Jesus suffer the worst violence on the cross? The logic goes that, as disciples of Jesus, we should similarly submit to the suffering of domestic abuse. God will use our suffering to mature us as Christians, or to be a good example to our boyfriend or husband, to win them over. These notions have nothing to do with the biblical image of a God who loves us compassionately, with kindness, mercy, grace and justice. Neither do they align with the biblical concept of suffering as we see demonstrated in Jesus and his work on the cross.

God is honest about the painful reality of suffering and violence in our world. The Bible tells us that God created us to live in peace and harmony with each other. But because of evil and sin there is suffering until Jesus returns and restores his followers to new life in the fullness of peace and God's love (Matt. 24:21; John 14:27; 1 Cor. 11:26; Rev. 21:3-4). It is important to recognise that while the Bible teaches us that suffering is part of life before Jesus returns, it reveals strongly that suffering is not God's ideal. Often it is brought about by evil and human sin—which means that inevitably all people will experience pain that is a result of another person's bad decisions and choices.

> God is honest about the painful reality of suffering and violence in our world.

Is God calling me to suffer in an abusive relationship?

Throughout the Bible, when God asks people to do things that will cause them suffering, it's in the interest of justice, righteousness and goodness. Submitting to domestic abuse does not lead to the fruit of God's love and therefore we are not called to remain in these situations. Nor does it lead to the abusive person's repentance or redemption, rather it enables the sin of abuse to continue. This is exactly what Jesus puts an end to in his suffering on the cross. God encourages us to promote healthy relationships and to have strong boundaries against people who are abusive. God only calls us to suffer in ways that are redemptive, and remaining in an abusive relationship is firmly against God's good plans for us.

The cross is an invitation to freedom, not suffering

The cross is about freedom: liberating people who are oppressed, marginalised and abused so they can enter into the full life as one in relationship with a loving God. The God of the Bible is one who suffers for us at the hands of men with power, who knowingly kill an innocent Jesus. The freedom Jesus offers by willingly submitting to the men who crucify him—and by God's resurrection of Jesus—is the opportunity for everyone to claim their new identity in the full life of God.

We do not need to submit to, or experience, suffering in order to help Jesus' work on the cross. *What Jesus did in his life, death and resurrection is complete. It is finished.* That is the beauty of it! Jesus chose to submit to the men who murdered him and God chose to redeem this unjust act by bringing Jesus back to life. And in so doing, to invite us to enter into the fullness of life with God and to be healed and free from bondage in God's perfect love and acceptance.

Conclusion

And yet, suffering still remains in this world until Jesus returns, and following Jesus is *in part* a call to share in the suffering of Christ. So if Jesus completed God's work to free us from all oppression and abuse through the resurrection of the crucified Christ, why—and in what ways—are we to share in Jesus' suffering?

First, we must remember that Jesus' suffering was complete (we can't add to it in any way!), we do not need to suffer to complete the work of the cross.

Secondly, we know that the Bible tells us we will experience suffering in the world due to evil and human sin. As we saw earlier, the Bible clarifies that domestic abuse is always a form of sin. It is a choice where one person uses power and control over another person in harmful ways. It is exactly this kind of sin—this injustice of abuse against women—that caused Jesus to die on the cross and God to resurrect him to life.

Thirdly, we must be clear that Jesus chose the violence of the cross. As God, Jesus could have easily avoided the cross,

> We do not need to suffer to complete the work of the cross.

but he chose to submit to the men who wanted to murder him. *Domestic abuse is not a choice on the part of the victim.* It is a choice made by the person who acts abusively and thus is an act of sin, which God seeks to redeem through the cross and resurrection to free the abused. Jesus' resurrection means that justice and peace have the final say. Jesus suffered *for sin*, but abuse victims suffer *because of sin*.

Finally, while followers of Jesus are called to enter into suffering as he did, it is a call to engage in *redemptive suffering*. Suffering domestic abuse is not in the interests of justice, righteousness or goodness. Christian leaders who encourage women to remain in abusive marriages are complicit in ongoing domestic abuse and should be held to account for this complicit behaviour.

The suffering that Jesus speaks about does not apply to those who experience domestic abuse, we are not called to submit to abuse, but to engage in *safe* procedures of standing up to those who commit sin by abusing them (Matthew 18:15-17; Luke 17:3).

TOP TIP

We are not called to submit to abuse. Suffering domestic abuse is not in the interest of justice, righteousness or goodness.

Notes

By Ally Kern

CHAPTER 25

Is it Biblical if I Leave or Divorce an Abusive Partner?

Divorce and remarriage happens all the time in the Bible

You may have heard from the church that the Bible says divorce is a sin, and only acceptable in the case of adultery or physical abandonment. For those who have experienced the anxiety, fear and even terror of being abused by a partner, the possibility of separation and divorce can often be a life-saving one. So if God is good and loving, committed to justice, and particularly cares for the vulnerable, how then can we understand God's teaching on divorce in the Bible? Is it even an option? And if so, in what circumstances? As we've discussed earlier, God defends the rights of the marginalised and abused—which is why God permits divorce throughout the Bible, including the case of abuse.

The reality in both the Old and New Testament is that followers of God were indeed separating and divorcing. Not just a few times, but as part of a social norm— although it certainly wasn't as common as it is today in Western culture. Scripture offers a practical solution for insufferable marriages: a certificate of divorce (Exodus

21; Deut. 24:1; Is. 50:1). Moses and the Prophets allowed divorce certificates to be initiated by either men or women based on the grounds for divorce outlined in Exodus 21:10-11—for the failure to provide food, clothing, and conjugal love—and in Deuteronomy 24:1 for sexual unfaithfulness. Women whose husbands had physically abandoned them were also given certificates of divorce, in order to protect their right to remarry and not be forced back into marriage with the spouses who had mistreated and abandoned them in case they returned.

> Jesus confirms that divorce for adultery and sexual immorality is scriptural, while Paul accepts neglect and physical abandonment as reasonable causes for divorce.

But didn't Jesus say divorce only in the case of adultery and abandonment?

In the New Testament Jesus confirms that divorce for adultery and sexual immorality is scriptural, while Paul accepts neglect and physical abandonment as reasonable causes for divorce (he bases his view of marital obligations on Exodus 21). Notably, Jesus does not directly speak to neglect, and Paul does not address adultery as a cause for divorce—although we tend to assume both are fine with either. Neither do Jesus or Paul directly confront the issue of abuse within marriage. Many biblical scholars assume—with relative confidence—that the absence of this discussion is due to the common understanding of the Jews that the law of the time had historically allowed for divorce due to abuse.

When the Pharisees ask Jesus a *specific* question about one *particular* context of divorce—allowing it for any reason at all, such as a wife burning her husband's dinner—Jesus says no to such divorce (Matt. 19:3-8). But importantly he isn't saying no to divorce in all circumstances.

Jesus says that men, who had power and privilege over their wives within ancient Greco-Roman culture (and still throughout most of the world today), should love their wives and not divorce unless adultery has occurred. So again, we see that Jesus isn't saying that divorce should *never* happen, but that the full context must be taken into account—especially the needs of the partner with less power: women. Jesus in particular, in addressing the husband, is affirming that he should protect his more vulnerable spouse and treat her with respect as a person. He is saying that by discarding a wife through divorce without a viable, biblical reason is tantamount to committing adultery. Jesus says no to men divorcing their wives when it would ultimately be an act of abuse. Jesus' stance then demonstrates God's firm commitment to protect women from being mistreated.

When Jesus and Paul are addressing the discussion of divorce in the New Testament, then, they are not getting into a debate about all the forms of divorce allowed in the Old Testament. They are simply speaking to the *new* idea presented by the Pharisees and the predominant Greco-Roman culture surrounding the Jews, that one could divorce one's spouse for *any reason* at all. In addition to protecting women, this also illustrates God's heart for marriage to be a safe place for a husband and wife to live together in love.

God initiates his own divorce!

While God's heart is for healing and reconciliation of marriages, the restoration of a biblical marriage is impossible when the abusive spouse does not repent or change. We must recognize the biblical grounds for divorce are intentionally created to protect oppressed, vulnerable and abused women (Exodus 21:10-11; Deut. 24:1; Is. 50:1; Matt. 19:3-8). Though God designed marriage to be a lifelong union, God himself divorces Israel for her hard heart after she refuses to repent and change her sinful behaviour—three times this is mentioned in Scripture (Isa. 50:1; 54:6-7; Jer. 3). In fact, this is what Jesus refers to when speaking to the Pharisees about divorce being allowed due to 'hard-heartedness'. This illustration of how seriously God views a relationship with his people continues in the New Testament, on an individual's level, as God calls people to repent of their sin in order to be in relationship with him (Luke 13:3; Matt. 3:2, 10-12; Acts 3:19).

The restoration of a biblical marriage is impossible when the abusive spouse does not repent or change.

Scripture demonstrates, then, that while God offers unconditional love, he does not offer unconditional relationship to those who will not repent and change. Our sin separates us not only from God, but also from each other, as in the case of abuse within marriage where the wife is dehumanized through her husband's sin. Marital intimacy, trust, fellowship and warmth cannot exist where there are fear, threats, intimidation, bullying and disrespect of one's thoughts, feelings, body, or personhood. A marriage without boundaries or conditions to protect those within the marriage and uphold God's design of marriage is not psychologically or spiritually healthy, and it is not biblical. The church and followers of Christ would do well to remember that there is no fear in love (1 John 4:18), and be prepared to support women suffering from domestic violence to remove themselves from psychologically, spiritually and physically unsafe husbands who refuse to repent and demonstrate change.

Once the biblical vows of marriage have been broken by abuse, neglect, adultery or abandonment, the wife is free to pursue divorce and remarriage to another man, just as the biblical divorce certificates always said, "You are now free to marry anyone you wish" (Deut. 24:1-4; Ex. 21:10; Ezekiel 16; Jer. 3:8; 1 Cor. 7:15, 39; Matt. 5:31-32).

But doesn't God hate divorce?

The Bible demonstrates that it is the abusive, adulterous or neglectful spouse who has broken the marriage vows and sinned against his spouse. Jesus certainly encourages forgiveness, but also recognizes and allows for divorce when a spouse has repeatedly broken their marriage vows and does not repent (reform their behaviour). It is certainly a biblical option for the wronged spouse to forgive and slowly consider reconciliation with a spouse who has genuinely repented and gone through a serious process of change over an extended period of time. However, because of God's heart for marriage to be a loving commitment for both partners, when an abusive spouse continues to refuse to acknowledge his sin and demonstrate accountable change in the long run, the Bible affirms the Old Testament law which gave the right to initiate divorce to the neglected or abused spouse. *God uses divorce as a tool for freedom for victims.*

While it is true that followers of Christ acknowledge suffering as part of their journey, we have also seen that suffering is to be redemptive, which is not the case with abusive spouses. Jesus also strongly condemns violence, and Scripture affirms protecting the victim of any form of domestic abuse. As Malachi 2:16 firmly declares, '"The man who hates and divorces his wife," says the LORD, the God of Israel, "does violence to the one he should protect".' God hates it when a husband acts hatefully towards his wife by divorcing her for no reason. God also hates the suffering that divorce can cause, but acknowledges that divorce may be the only way for an abused wife—and her children—to be safe, to heal and to flourish. The Bible thus protects an abused wife by allowing for her to pursue divorce.

 TOP TIP Once the biblical vows are broken by abuse, neglect, adultery or abandonment, the wife is free to pursue divorce and remarriage to another man.

Notes

By Esther Sweetman

CHAPTER 26

Spiritual Abuse

Many survivors of domestic abuse have also experienced spiritual abuse. This may have been perpetrated by their spouses or by church leaders or members.

Thirtyone:eight (formally known as CCPAS - The Churches Child Protection Advisory Service), an independent safeguarding Christian charity in the UK has produced papers and publications on this topic.

In their publication entitled *I Want to Understand Spiritual Abuse*[1], Thirtyone:eight uses the definition of spiritual abuse as was outlined by Lisa Oakley(2013) in Oakley & Kinmond[2]

'*Spiritual abuse is coercion and control of one individual by another in a spiritual context. The target experiences spiritual abuse as a deeply emotional personal attack. This abuse may include:- manipulation and exploitation, enforced accountability, censorship of decision making, requirements for secrecy and silence, pressure to conform, misuse of scripture or the pulpit to control behaviour, requirement of obedience to the abuser, the suggestion that the abuser has a 'divine' position, isolation from others, especially those external to the abusive context.*'

They go on to explain,

'To begin with, it is important to understand that spiritual abuse is a form of psychological and emotional abuse that takes place within a faith context. Sufferers therefore experience being controlled, coerced and pressurised within churches and places of worship.'

The wheel on the next page which has been produced by Safe Havens Interfaith Partnerships Against Domestic Violence[3] outlines the different forms spiritual abuse can take.

Elements that may feel very familiar to survivors include using scripture or traditions:

- to encourage us to forgive
- to keep the relationship together
- to sacrifice ourselves for the relationship
- to excuse or minimize the abuse
- to remain silent or accept the suffering
- to impose gender roles that are abusive or coercive
- to assert authority, to reinforce male privilege
- to encourage us to submit
- to give commands or to punish us
- to justify abuse or blame us

Within relationships, spiritual abuse happens when one person misrepresents scripture in order to control and create dependence in the other person. This can happen between husband and wife and can happen in churches where church leaders encourage the victim of abuse to remain in an abusive situation or be ostracized by their community.

According to CCPAS, one way which can help prevent spiritual abuse is through **empowerment**.

Empowerment is encouraging individuals, within spiritual contexts, to develop autonomy. Healthy spiritual contexts encourage people to develop as individuals who can think for themselves and are able to express disagreement or concern.

What that might mean for survivors is to seek out churches and church leaders who have an understanding of domestic abuse, and knowledge about how to address it appropriately when it becomes evident within their congregation and its members.

It might mean that we all need to educate ourselves on what the bible has to say about domestic abuse and divorce due to abuse, and to stand firm in the knowledge that:

Any form of abuse, then, is unacceptable behaviour which directly defies God's calling for Christ-followers to relate to each other in love. The person who abuses is sinning, the victim who wants to leave is not in sin. While not everyone has the ability to leave an abusive partner, it is not wrong to attempt to do so if possible, the Bible encourages victims to seek safety (Proverbs 22:3 and 27:12; 1 Samuel 20; Luke 4:28-29; Acts 9:23-25; Matthew 18:15-17).

We all need to educate ourselves on what the bible has to say about domestic abuse and divorce due to abuse.

"God acts clearly through the life and death of Jesus to take an ultimate stance against all forms of violence, oppression, marginalization, and abuse, declaring that 'God is love' and God's love will not stand passively or silently when women are abused (1 John 4:8)." Please refer to Chapter 23: What Does the Bible Really have to say about Domestic Abuse? by Ally Kern.

Once the biblical vows of marriage have been broken by abuse, neglect, adultery or abandonment, the wife is free to pursue divorce and remarriage to another man, just as the biblical divorce certificates always said, "You are now free to marry anyone you wish" (Deut. 24:1-4; Ex. 21:10; Ezekiel 16:16; Jer. 3:8; 1 Cor. 7:15, 39; Matt. 5:31-32). Please refer to Chapter 25: Is it Biblical if I Leave or Divorce an Abusive Partner by Ally Kern.

Spiritual And Religious Abuse
Using Scripture, Traditions, and Cultural Norms to Assert Power and Control

Asserting Authority
Using Scripture, traditions, or cultural norms to impose gender roles that are abusive or coercive, to assert authority, to reinforce male privilege, to encourage you to submit, to give commands, or to punish you.

Prolonging Abusive Relationships
Using Scripture, traditions, or cultural norms to encourage you to forgive, to keep the relationship together, to sacrifice yourself for the relationship, to excuse or minimize the abuse, to remain silent, or to accept suffering.

Isolation
Isolating you from your faith community by not allowing you to participate in services or events, by silencing you when you are there, by moving the family from congregation to congregation, or by forcing you to attend services in a different faith community.

Controlling Sexuality and Reproduction
Using Scripture, traditions, or cultural norms to force you to have sex or unprotected sex, to deny or force family planning, to participate in polygamous marriage or genital mutilation, to have sex or be married at a young age, to be in an arranged or forced marriage.

Using Community Coercion
Working through clergy or lay leader, or friends or family from your faith community, to put pressure on you to stay in the relationship or to put up with abuse. Coercion may take the form of letters or phone calls on the abuser's behalf, comments in social settings, etc.

Using Children
Using Scripture, traditions, or cultural norms to arrange and force marriage for teens, to value male over female children, to use girls as commodities for bride prize or dowry, to sell young girls as commodities, to force you to raise children in another faith or no faith.

Restricting Access to or Use of Health Care
Using Scripture, traditions or cultural norms to force you to forego regular check ups, family planning, medications, emergency medical care, or to neglect medical care for your children.

Blaming The Victim
Using Scripture, traditions, or cultural norms to blame you and justify abuse because you are female, sinful, and the weaker vessel, estranged from God, not created in God's image, created to be man's servant, unclean, polluted, defiled.

Safe Havens Interfaith Partnership (2014)

189

Be empowered by knowing what the Bible really says about domestic abuse.

References

1 The Churches' Child Protection Advisory Service (CCPAS) (2015). *I Want to Understand Spiritual Abuse* files.ccpas.co.uk/documents/Help-SpiritualAbuse%20(2015).pdf (accessed 5/10/18).

2 Oakley, L.R. & Kinmond, K. S. (2013) *Breaking the silence on spiritual abuse*. Palgrave McMillan

3 Safe Havens Interfaith Partnership (2014). *Spiritual and Religious Abuse Wheel*. Reprinted with Permission. docs.wixstatic.com/ugd/991f52_1ad03da183cf4f4db1e395f6d5059685.pdf (accessed on 5/10/18).

Notes

By Esther Sweetman

CHAPTER 27

Faith, Justice and Domestic Abuse

How does your faith influence your understanding of justice in the face of domestic abuse?

This was the question that a researcher from the Gender and Violence Centre of Bristol University asked me. I went on a journey to answer this question, and I ask you to walk with me.

When we talk about justice, we infer that an injustice exists; someone has been wronged. When we talk about domestic abuse, the victim has been, among other things, humiliated and degraded – robbed of their dignity and humanity – that is part of the "wrong" that has been committed.

The reality of domestic abuse is unspeakable, so unspeakable that churches, friends and family often don't want to *speak* about it. It is much easier for us to brush it under the carpet, pretend it's not happening, and put the onus on the woman to take responsibility for her spouse's abuse. This requires her to repeatedly forgive so that everyone else can avoid potential conflict and uncomfortable feelings in the church community; but what does the bible say God requires of us in this situation?

To act justly and to love mercy and to walk humbly with your God. Micah 6:8 (NIV)

More often than not, when domestic abuse occurs in churches, we see forgiveness and mercy for the husband as a priority without even considering what justice for the wife might mean; the long-term consequences of the abuse for the wife are not considered. And the ramifications for the wife, if the perpetrator is not called to account or held responsible for his behaviour, are not even contemplated.

As Christians, it is so easy to love mercy and forget about justice. We all want mercy for our own shortcomings, so we are at the forefront of offering mercy to others – which is admirable. But what about seeking justice for those who have been wronged? This aspect of God's call on our lives is often overlooked. So what does seeking justice in the face of domestic abuse look like?

What is the Biblical understanding of justice?

Justice can often come with negative connotations: retribution, vengeance, payback etc. Interestingly, however, after having worked with domestic abuse survivors, I have not seen one woman indicate they want their spouse to be punished. No one has wanted to retaliate or to seek vengeance – this is not the type of justice survivors want. The majority want their experience to be validated and the truth of the wrongdoing acknowledged and acted upon appropriately. Not surprisingly, the biblical approach to justice is similar.

The biblical words for justice relate to righteousness: seeking what is right or seeking to make things right. It relates to fair judgement and to love and healing. As Jim Wallis puts it in *The (Un)Common Good: How the Gospel Brings Hope to a World Divided,*

"One of the clearest and most holistic words for justice is the Hebrew shalom, which means both 'justice' and 'peace.' Shalom includes 'wholeness,' or everything that makes for people's well being, security, and, in particular, the restoration of relationships that have been broken. Justice, therefore, is about repairing broken relationships both with other people and to structures — of courts and punishments, money and economics, land and resources, and kings and rulers. The deeply biblical idea of shalom is the reason justice always has to be social.

"So justice, most simply, means putting things right again — fixing, repairing and restoring broken relationships. Justice and righteousness are interrelated and are to be sought in social relationships and social structures. Christians are asked to make justice more possible in this world every day. Our justice lens for viewing and acting on any unjust situation in society should be looking at what's wrong and figuring out how to make it right. Seeking justice is as basic as that."

So what does this type of justice look like in the face of domestic violence and abuse in our church communities?

> As Christians, it is so easy to love mercy and forget about justice.

As a church, we need to consciously and intentionally take a stand for the victim. In many domestic violence cases, legal justice needs to be sought to protect victims and others, and when it is appropriate, churches need to support this process. The good news is that UK law is increasingly recognising different aspects of domestic abuse (such as the new coercive control law) and the natural consequence for criminal behaviour needs to be served. Yet legal systems have limits. Survivors of domestic abuse have to assess the emotional, psychological and health-related costs of manoeuvring through the legal system and going to court, especially considering, from a statistical point of view, they have a potentially small chance of legal justice being realised.

This is where the church needs to stand up and seek social and restorative justice for the victim. The leaders of the Church need to be role models; developing a moral and principled community and leading the way in signposting just behaviour in the face of injustice. We need to help others to understand what is wrong, and figure out how to make it right.

Not only must we walk alongside the victim of domestic abuse within our congregations with practical support, care and compassion, but God asks us to seek justice for her to make things right; to seek justice for her personally, and to seek justice for her within her community. Seeking to restore the victim's safety and sanity as well as her personal dignity, both within herself and in front of her community, is paramount. How do we do this?

We must ask ourselves, in every interaction we have with the victim, "Does our behaviour and do our words demonstrate understanding, compassion and support? Do they uphold the woman's safety, sanity and dignity?" In every interaction we have with the perpetrator we must ask the very same question: "Does our behaviour and do our words continue to uphold the woman's safety, sanity and dignity or do we remain complicit through silence, enabling the abusive behaviour to continue unchallenged?" We need to consider the messages our words and actions, or lack of them, are sending to both the victim and the perpetrator. And above all else, everything we do must be victim-centred, consulting her to ensure her safety, sanity and dignity in every action we take.

The leaders of the Church need to be role models; developing a moral and principled community.

Challenge the Perpetrator and Challenge Dismissive Attitudes.

But what stops us seeking justice for the victim as a priority? Are we brushing the issues under the carpet because confronting an abuser is "a bit awkward" and could create conflict? Do we see supporting the victim as "taking a rather uncomfortable stand"? We need to balance this awkwardness and discomfort against the reality of a woman's safety, sanity and dignity. Never forget; two women a week die due to domestic abuse in the UK. It is vital that we challenge the structures and attitudes in our individual churches, and with their members who may foster, ignore or, at times, ignorantly collude with domestic abuse.

According to the biblical blueprint, seeking justice for the victim of domestic abuse is of primary importance. However, after having worked with domestic abuse survivors in the church, one of the main stories I hear – repeatedly – is how church leaders and members of the congregation seek inappropriate mercy for the perpetrator over justice for the victim.

There can be a rush to forgive and show mercy to the abusive husband, unknowingly stamping on the wife's soul again and minimising the abusive behaviour. When this happens, we expand the disrespect experienced by the victim by ignoring the consequences of the harm done, and re-traumatize the victim by pretending a tearful "sorry" from the perpetrator can repair the scars from years of abuse. We falsely assume that the perpetrator's character can miraculously undergo a transformation without any call to account or any hard work to change their attitudes and actions.

> There can be a rush to forgive and show mercy to the abusive husband, unknowingly stamping on the wife's soul again and minimising the abusive behaviour.

Instead, "cheap forgiveness" is provided, and interaction with the perpetrator continues as if nothing untoward has occurred. This behaviour validates the perpetrator's actions by seemingly condoning the abuser's behaviour and attitude. It fosters an environment that encourages the abuser's fantasy that what he has done is not that bad, that his behaviour is justified and that the "victim" is the one with the problem. It lets him know that his actions have no consequences.

Of course we need to engage in support for the perpetrator, but only within the context of principled and tough actions. If it's safe for the woman, we need to have those tough conversations about the unacceptability of his behaviour, and understand that transformation is a long process that needs to be evaluated by changed behaviour and not sorrowful words. We should ask whether the perpetrator needs to be relieved of leadership roles within the church. And if it is impossible for both members of the couple to remain in the same church, our default should be that the perpetrator is asked to leave, not the victim. We must seek a covenant of accountability with the perpetrator, and communication with new churches needs to occur – churches need to work together to ensure the safety of their congregations. Progressing with the status quo and remaining neutral is no longer an option.

Restoration of Relationships

Church leaders and members often see restoration of the marital relationship as the primary goal, but when domestic abuse is occurring this is wrong and irresponsible. Trying to keep the marriage intact keeps the wife in a physically and/or mentally unsafe relationship and puts the onus on her to forgive, rather than requiring the abuser to demonstrate real change, or engage in any restitution or reparations. He experiences no consequences, and there is no motivating force to propel him to change.

Attempting to restore the relationship between the victim and perpetrator may not be physically or mentally safe and overlooks the long-term consequences experienced by victims of abuse. Restorative justice should therefore be about seeking to restore the victim's relationship with the church. Did the church fail to believe her? Did the church sweep the abuse under the carpet? Was she shunned by the community? Did she lose her own faith, not because of the abuse, but because of the indifference and weakness of her church leaders and community to do what is right? If the church is guilty of any of this, we need to repent and change behaviour and engage in purposeful actions to restore the relationship of the victim with her church community.

Church leaders have the stature necessary to provide meaningful outward signs (signals to the community without needing to reveal private details), allowing the community to know that this woman remains in right relationship with God and in right relationship with the church.

> **Justice is about restoration and healing for those who are oppressed.**

These actions can thereby restore her dignity inwardly and publicly in the midst of her church community – after having experienced domestic abuse and often after experiencing the very public subsequent divorce.

Justice is about restoration and healing for those who are oppressed. Church leaders and church members have a role to play in seeking justice, healing and restoration for those members of the church who have experienced domestic abuse. God has shown his people what is right in the face of oppression, in the face of those who have experienced domestic abuse. The blueprint to right relationships and to healing has been outlined for us. Take a stand for the victim, challenge the perpetrator and contest dismissive attitudes, while always seeking the safety, sanity and dignity of the victim with your words and behaviour.

Thank you for taking a walk with me to answer this question. My hope is that you will now be able to walk alongside a domestic abuse survivor, seeking justice for her in your own church community. For, to paraphrase Micah,

He has already shown us, O mortals, what is good and right.

 TOP TIP Find a church community that will prioritize your safety, sanity and dignity.

Reference
Wallis, J. (2014). *The (Un)Common Good: How the Gospel Brings Hope to a World Divided*. Grand Rapids: Brazos Press.

By Esther Sweetman

CHAPTER 28

Forgiveness after Abuse

Too many books or talks on forgiveness can be summarised in four words, 'bitterness bad, forgiveness good.' They usually contain anecdotes that feature wretched people caught up in a cycle of bitterness and blessed saints who have managed to forgive their tormentor. These talks do not usually discuss *situations* of significant abuse but nevertheless are directed towards *survivors* of significant abuse. The homilies may refer to forgiveness as a process, but rarely acknowledge traumatised and struggling individuals who are barely surviving their day, let alone having the remotest capacity to venture into the world of forgiving their perpetrator.

The Christian anecdote most often used to highlight the amazing capacity to forgive is that of Corrie Ten Boom, who managed to shake the hand of her concentration camp guard years after her release. The reason why this anecdote should not be held up as an example for abused women to forgive their perpetrators is that the circumstances are not equatable. Although Corrie Ten Boom's experience was horrific, her offer of forgiveness was expressed in a 5 second handshake to a man who was repentant and converted. He was not currently stalking her, he was not slandering her weekly to her church community, she did not have to co-parent with him while he continued to abuse her. The example of Corrie Ten Boom is an inappropriate equivalence.

The False Dichotomy

Sermons that contain an exhortation to "forgive or else fall into the abyss of bitterness" are based on a false dichotomy where forgiveness is at one end of the spectrum and bitterness at the other. The road to forgiveness is made so narrow, and the path so pre-determined, that it creates huge restrictions as to who can pass through, and the mode of transport they are allowed to use. The assumption that it is the lack of forgiveness which causes an extended recovery is evident, while there is very little understanding that the long-term effects of abuse and trauma are actually what cause a protracted recovery.

These long term consequences of domestic abuse can include PTSD, depression and chronic physical ill-health. In addition, if the survivor has managed to leave the man who is abusing her, she may not have any income or access to finances. She may need to find work, move house and parent distraught children while simultaneously managing her own recovery. What might look like bitterness might simply be exhaustion from the massive effort it takes to create a new life, find a new job and new home, and support children in a new family structure, all the while still recovering oneself and potentially still being abused by an ex-partner who doesn't want to let go of their victim willingly. These are just some of the reasons why forgiving a perpetrator may move quite low on the priority list for a survivor.

Breaking out of the prison of guilt and shame in which this false dichotomy holds survivors prisoner, and unchaining them from the implication that their recovery is directly connected to their ability to forgive their perpetrator, has the capacity to enable a survivor to move forward in amazing and unexpected ways.

Shattering Hurt

Stephen Cherry, author of *Healing Agony: Re-Imagining Forgiveness* (2012), explains that the historical context to a forgiveness story is of great importance. He outlines four levels of hurt: *trivial, serious, significant and shattering*. Cherry explains that the level of hurt endured makes a difference as to the kind of response that is possible by the survivor. Victims of abuse usually experience a *shattering* level of hurt that undermines their health, integrity and identity. Cherry asserts that a person who has experienced this level of hurt should never be asked to extend easy or cheap forgiveness.

Cherry highlights the fact that requiring quick and easy forgiveness colludes with the oppressors, aggressors and violators. When there is too much tolerance, when hurts are more than trivial, we inhibit emotions and reactions that tell us something is wrong and unacceptable. It causes the survivor to bury their emotions, which can lead to even greater depression or physical illnesses. In addition, if someone is required to forgive too easily or quickly, the ramification can be severe as the

> **What might look like bitterness might simply be exhaustion from the massive effort it takes to create a new life.**

perpetrator will experience no consequences and may continue to abuse the victim or others.

It is also important to understand the distinction between forgiveness and reconciliation. Reconciliation may not ever be appropriate between a survivor and their abuser. Strong boundaries may need to be set by the survivor to ensure that their safety, sanity and dignity is safeguarded into the future. Neither is forgiveness about expecting the survivor to excuse the abusive behaviour so that no one in the church would have to address a difficult situation.

The journey of forgiveness needs to begin from a place of safety.

So addressing the question of forgiveness is generally the wrong place to start with survivors of abuse. The journey of forgiveness needs to begin from a place of safety, both physically and psychologically. Attention to recovery and healing from the wrong that was done and the abuse that was suffered needs to come first. The role of the church in these situations is to provide support and to seek justice for the survivor, before seeking the survivor's offer of forgiveness for the perpetrator.

The journey towards forgiveness can start when victims become aware of the longer-term damage done to them, and when they have friends, family and community supporting them in their recovery.

Misinterpreting the Lord's Prayer
The traditional understanding of forgiveness within the Christian worldview is usually informed by a misinterpretation of the Lord's Prayer, that is, that one has to forgive to be forgiven; as well as by the subsequent assumption that until one forgives, there will be no complete healing. This understanding encourages forgiveness based on the fear of God rather than inviting a forgiving approach through the grace of God. It reduces forgiveness to an impersonal transaction with God: I forgive to get forgiveness from God.

The wide acceptance of this traditional understanding of forgiveness within church communities can cause Christians to feel obliged to tell survivors *where they are going wrong in terms of forgiveness*, when they do not even know the full story of the person they are judging.

According to The Faith and Order Commission of the Church of England, who wrote *Forgiveness and Reconciliation in the Aftermath of Abuse* (Cocksworth, 2017), the words on forgiveness in the Lord's Prayer should be read as the prayer of the whole church - it is not asserting that God provides individual forgiveness based on an individual's ability to forgive others. It is a communal or collective prayer for the way we hope to be as a church, a community seeking to be forgiving. When we pray the Lord's Prayer individually, we are not making a statement of fact regarding the way God's forgiveness works or claiming that each of us must be completely and perfectly forgiving to receive forgiveness, rather we are indicating our participation in the prayer of the whole church as we strive to become a forgiving people.

How Churches Get it Wrong

People are often pushed to forgive their perpetrator because church leaders or members are scared or uncomfortable with the survivor's anger or distress. Anger is too often associated with revenge or bitterness and is not recognised as a powerful emotion that can be harnessed for good. It can give people the strength to stand up against horrific evil or everyday wrongs. It may have given the survivor the strength to leave their abusive situation. Cherry states that forgiveness requires the church community to risk becoming angry when they recognise injustice.

Not being able to forgive one's abuser does not necessarily equate to ongoing bitterness. It may indicate unresolved trauma, lack of support from one's community, an acknowledgement that justice has not been achieved or an awareness that the perpetrator remains unrepentant and continues to abuse. What an observer does not understand, when they encourage a survivor to forgive their abuser, is that after a confrontation or a separation, the abusive events may not be over, the perpetrator will often continue to abuse. Abuse and its consequences are rarely finite. You may be asking the survivor to continue to forgive in the face of ongoing abuse which can go on for years. This request is naive, unhealthy and painfully unjust. *'Holding forgiveness and justice in a properly balanced tension is a significant part of the task of formulating theologies that can inform the work of safeguarding from abuse and responding to it.'* (Cocksworth, 2017). Church leaders and members cannot remain in a state of denial and carry on as if nothing has happened, it only perpetuates the deceit and failure to seek justice.

Community Responsibility - Choose To Be An Event of Grace

Too often I have seen a finger of judgement pointing at a survivor of abuse because they have not reached a place of forgiveness. Side glances and whispers are common - "Why can't this person just get over it?" It might be helpful to remember that it is likely you have stepped into an abusive situation at a particular point in time, with the strength and reserves that have come to you from historically supportive relationships, with relatively strong self-esteem and a solid support system. An abused person has often experienced an onslaught of sustained verbal, psychological and/or physical abuse and isolation over a long period of time, abuse that was purposefully designed to break them down; and they DO get broken. Yet an onlooker expects that the survivor should have the same reserves and capacity to survive and cope and forgive as *they* would, and they are surprised, and potentially judgmental, when the survivor cannot.

None of us like to be thought of as judgmental but when we reflect on our own instinctive reactions when we hear a survivor's story, is there anything now that we would change? Instead of wondering why she is still struggling or why she doesn't heed your advice perhaps ask yourself "What I am doing to support this person on their journey towards forgiveness?", "Does my judgement or advice help them on their journey?" "Or does it break them down a little bit more?" It is always important to consider, "Do I have the right to speak into this person's life if I am unwilling or unable to demonstrate care, compassion and concrete support?"

It is challenging for Christians to understand that a forgiving heart is fostered over time, through the grace and healing of God demonstrated through his people, and that sometimes forgiveness can be the last step of healing from trauma rather than the first. Understanding forgiveness in this way shows that church communities must take their part in supporting a survivor on their road to forgiveness, walking alongside a victim in their pain and on their healing journey rather than standing above them with a superior attitude.

The deep wounds, permanent scars and heroic efforts of survivors should be recognised. Survivors need compassion and support from their community rather than judgemental attitudes and comments. From my work, I have observed that the healing process requires many events of grace that occur in God's time and through a supportive community. It is through loving relationships that transformation can occur and bring healing to hearts, souls and minds. *Choose to be an event of grace in a survivor's life.*

An Alternate Understanding of Forgiveness

I suggest a radically different paradigm or model to understand the trajectory of forgiveness for those who have been abused. I propose that the road to forgiving a perpetrator of abuse is necessarily wide and that the mode of transport to get there, and the length of the journey, is different for each survivor. It is possible that the harm done to a survivor is so severe that it may take years, or even decades, to reach a place of being open to consider forgiving; and that even a committed, loving Christian might never fully arrive at forgiveness. I suggest that respect, understanding and support be extended to survivors, by the church community, no matter where they find them on the road to forgiveness.

This alternative paradigm for forgiveness is less about encouraging survivors to say a 'magic' set of words that hold little internal meaning for them, and is more about acknowledging the incredible bravery exhibited by a survivor engaging in a sometimes painfully slow healing process. Offering forgiveness, in this paradigm, is the last point on the long road to recovery by the survivor and not the first.

This new paradigm suggests that it is only through healing grace, loving relationships, and the embrace of a caring and supportive community, that survivors may start the process of recovery which may one day allow them to forgive.

 TOP TIP Reach out to trusted family and friends who can be an event of grace in your life.

References

Cherry, Stephen. *Healing Agony: Re-Imagining Forgiveness.* (2012). London, New York: Continuum International Publishing Group.

Cocksworth,Christopher. *Forgiveness and Reconciliation in the Aftermath of Abuse.* (2017). London: Church House Publishing.

SUPPORTING RESTORED

We hope that this handbook has been a useful resource to you and to anyone else it has helped as a result. Restored is always extremely appreciative of its volunteers and those who organise fundraising events which allow us to continue the work we do. We are grateful for every small donation because without your help we would not exist!

Regular Giving

Regular giving on a monthly basis is the best way to support Restored. This enables us to plan effectively and use resources strategically where we believe they will make the most impact. If you would like to support this way please set up a regular gift here *www.give.net/ Restored*. Of course we understand that right now that may be impossible for you, but later on you may want to consider it, or suggest it to friends or family.

Fundraising Events

Fundraising events are another option to support Restored that can be fun and you can do with friends and family. They do not necessarily have to be big. You may want to do something to raise funds that will stretch you (sky diving, wing walking, running) or something less arduous such as a bake sale, dinner party, or host a clothes swishing event (bring good clothes that you no longer wear and people buy them). If you would like to do a fundraising event then please get in touch with us as we would love to be encouraged by you, support you where we can, and pray for you. Check out Restored's Fundraising pack for more options here *www.restoredrelationships .org/resources/info/108/*

Making a will

Wills may not be something we talk very much about but it is important to do. Writing a will gives you the opportunity to think through what assets you currently have and how you wish them to be distributed after your death. Death is a reality, we all die. We simply don't like talking about it and hope that it is a very long way off. Making a list of your assets and who you would like them to go to is important. If you have bigger items such as a house, car, or high value jewellery you will need to think through how this will be distributed. Do you want specific items to go to different people? A percentage of all your assets? You may not think you have much at all but do not underestimate the value of the small things which may be of huge sentimental value to a relative. While you are planning your will, would you consider leaving something to Restored?

There is plenty of help available to write a will and you may need a solicitor's help in putting the will together. Take a look at Restored's Legacy pack here for more information: *www.restoredrelationships .org/resources/info/145/*

Other Areas of Support

It may be that you cannot give financially right now to the work of Restored but there are other ways to support us too. Firstly, pray for survivors of abuse, the staff and volunteers of Restored, and the work we do. We are challenging power and control and are aware that this is a huge issue to address. We are grateful for prayers as we head into this arena.

Another way to support us is to like, share or retweet posts on social media. Restored is on Instagram, Facebook, Twitter and LinkedIn. Do find us and like our pages and share our posts so that more people know we exist and can use our excellent resources, like the church pack. *www.restoredrelationships.org/resources/ info/51/*

Thank you

We are so grateful for each individual that supports Restored, in whatever way you do. Thank you.

Mandy Marshall
Co-Founder and Co-Director, Restored

Restored
Ending Violence Against Women

INTRODUCING THE AUTHORS

Robin McKay Bell is the co-author of *Finding Work After* 40, a careers book published by Bloomsbury. He is also the Founder and Programme Leader at *Room for Work*, a charity that delivers an employability skills course for mature people who are struggling to regain employment. The course has helped hundreds of women return to work after a crisis or a long absence from the workplace. (www.roomforwork.org)

Betsy de Thierry is a psychotherapist, teacher, trainer, pastor and author of many books on children and trauma. She is the CEO of the Trauma Recovery Centre (multi site trauma therapy centres), Therapeutic Mentoring Rooms in schools and senior church leader/ founder of Freedom Centre UK a church in Bath, UK. (www.betsytraininguk.co.uk) She is also a mum of four sons aged 10-22.

Nikki Dhillon Keane is a counsellor, consultant and trainer who has spent many years working with survivors of domestic abuse. She is a member of the Catholic Bishops Conference Domestic Abuse Working Group and is the author of *"Domestic Abuse in Church Communities: A Safe Pastoral Response"* (Redemptorist Publications). You can contact her at nikkidhillonk@rcdow.org.uk.

Jan Eubanks is currently a social worker in a London Borough. Throughout her professional career she has navigated through roles where advocacy and justice are at the core of their function and has worked as an Independent Domestic Violence Advocate, Family Support Worker, Corporate Equalities & Human Rights Office, SEN Special Support worker and Play Leader. She has a vast breadth of knowledge on issues relating to domestic abuse, child protection, human trafficking/modern day slavery, mental capacity assessments, deprivation of liberty safeguards (DoLS) and general care/support needs under the Care Act 2014.

Susie Flashman Jarvis is passionate about supporting individuals to bring about change in their lives. She works as an executive coach and counsellor with businesses and individuals (thebespokecoach.com). She is a writer and speaker, and as an ambassador for Restored, highlights the need for support for those caught up in abusive situations.

Miriam Hargreaves has worked with women involved in street prostitution in East London, as a counsellor for Women's Aid (with domestic abuse survivors in the UK), in pastoral counselling with women in the local church and now works with Beyond the Streets on Beyond Support, the phone support service for women who sell sex in the UK.

Deborah Hewitt worked at a local Christians Against Poverty Debt Centre for 5 years heading up their CAP Money Course and as a Licensed Money Coach. She has volunteered for many years with Citizens Advice, with a special interest in finance issues.

Faye Hurley is an award-winning entrepreneur, motivational speaker and coach, who works with female entrepreneurs. Ten years ago, following multiple toxic relationships, Faye realised the key to *attracting* and *receiving* love & success was to love herself first, which unveiled the belief that she was born *inherently worthy*. As she embodied this belief, the love and life she had dreamt of as a child, became her reality. She now helps others to do the same.

Ally Kern is a survivor of domestic abuse. As an Adjunct Professor in Practical Theology at Azusa Pacific University and a Ph.D. candidate at Claremont School of Theology, she developed cutting-edge research integrating feminist and pastoral theology, psychology, neuroscience, and women's studies to create faith-based resources for women to heal from relationship abuse. She brings two decades of pastoral ministry to her work as a speaker, writer, and advocate for women's flourishing and the end of violence against women and girls. Go to www.allykern.com to learn more about her work and to find free resources on domestic abuse and gender-based violence.

Mandy Marshall is the Co-Founder and Co-Director of Restored. Mandy is an international speaker and trainer on issues of domestic abuse, violence against women and gender based violence in the Christian context. Mandy worships at St Stephen's Church, Twickenham and plays hockey for her local club, Richmond.

 Lucy McDonald is the Global Operations Coordinator for Generosity Path. Alongside this she works for Goldsmith's University facilitating their online MA in Domestic Violence and Sexual Abuse. She also volunteers for Restored and works on the National Domestic Violence Helpline.

 Esther Sweetman is a qualified counsellor, social researcher and has trained in theological studies. She has held various roles in the helping profession over many years as well as conducting research for organizations and managing a functional/psychological assessment centre. Currently, she takes the lead in the survivors work at Restored and has coordinated Restored's online Survivors' Network for the last 3 years.

 Mary Waring is founder of Wealth for Women Limited (WfW), a boutique financial advisory firm specialising in independent financial advice to women going through divorce. Typically, my clients feel overwhelmed by the prospect of making financial decisions, since her husband has managed the finances during the marriage. WfW provides confidence clarity and peace of mind about her financial future (www.wealthforwomen.biz).

 Louisa Whitney practised as a family lawyer for 13 years before qualifying as a family mediator. She found the work of a mediator more constructive in helping couples who were separating to address the issues they faced and in 2013 left her work as a solicitor to set up her own family mediation practice, LKW Family Mediation. She also supervises and trains other mediators and offers training to any professionals working with separated couples. She is passionate about helping separating couples to minimise the effects of their separation on their children.

RESOURCES:
FURTHER SUPPORT AND INFORMATION

For Urgent Support

- **Emergency Services: 999**
- **UK National Domestic Violence Helpline: 0808 2000 247** (24 hours a day)
- **Samaritans Helpline: Freephone 116 123** (UK & Eire 24 hours a day)
- **Women's Aid:** www.womensaid.org.uk
- **Refuge:** www.refuge.org.uk

What is Domestic Abuse?

Helpful Christian books and leaflets

- **Violence in Families: What Every Christian Needs to Know.** Al Miles (2002) Augsburg Press.
- **Addressing Domestic Violence in the Church.** Bob & Helga Edwards (2017) CreateSpace Independent Publishing.
- **Unholy Charade: Unmasking the Domestic Abuser in the Church.** Jeff Crippen (2015) Justice Keepers Publishing.
- **Family and Friends Guide to Domestic Violence: How to Listen, Talk and Take Action when Someone You Care About is Being Abused.** Elaine Weiss. (2004). Volcano Press.
- **I Want to Understand Spiritual Abuse.** The Churches' Child Protection Advisory Service (CCPAS) (2015). https://files.ccpas.co.uk/documents/Help-SpiritualAbuse%20(2015).pdf
- **No Place for Abuse.** Nancy Nason-Clark and Catherine Clark-Kroeger (2011). IVP USA

Helpful books

- **Why Does He Do That? Inside the Minds of Angry and Controlling Men.** Lundy Bancroft (2003) Penguin Random House.

- **Should I Stay or Should I Go? A Guide to Knowing if Your Relationship Can–and Should–be Saved.** Lundy Bancroft and JA Patrissi (2011) Penguin Random House.
- **Coercive Control: How Men Entrap Women in Personal Life.** Evan Stark (2009) Oxford University Press.
- **When Love Hurts: A Woman's Guide to Understanding Abuse in Relationships.** Jill Cory and Karen McAndless-Davis (2016) Penguin Random House.
- **Living with the Dominator: A book about the Freedom Programme.** Pat Craven (2008) Freedom Publishing.
- **Power And Control: Why Charming Men Can Make Dangerous Lovers.** Sandra Horley (2002) Vermilion.
- **Operation Lighthouse.** Luke and Ryan Hart (2018). Coco Awareness Ltd.
- **At Therapy's End.** Susie Flashman Jarvis (2015). Instant Apostle.
- **Scars Across Humanity.** Elaine Storkey (2018). IVP Academic

Managing the Practical Realities after Leaving a Male Abuser

Accomodation
- **Refuge** www.refuge.org.uk
- **Women's Aid** www.womensaid.org.uk
- **LAWA: Latin American Women's Aid** runs two UK refuges by and for Latin American and BME women and children fleeing gender-based violence www.lawadv.org.uk/en/
- **Shelter:** For housing advice: www.shelter.org.uk 0808 800 4444

Legal Support and Protective Orders
- **Women's Aid** (to find an Independent Domestic Violence Advocate) www.womensaid.org.uk
- **Rights of Women** free legal advice by phone www.rightsofwomen.org.uk
- **Law Society** (to find a solicitor) 020 7320 5650 www.solicitors.lawsociety.org.uk
- **Legal Aid Agency** 0345 345 4 345
- **Forced Marriage Unit Helpline** 0207 008 0151
- **National Centre for Domestic Violence** www.ncdv.org.uk 0800 970 2070
- **Community Legal Service Direct** www.clsdirect.org.uk 0845 345 345

Protection from Stalking (UK)
- **National Stalking Helpline 0808 802 0300** www.stalkinghelpline.org
- **Network for Surviving Stalking** www.nss.org.uk
- **Action Scotland Against Stalking:** www.scotlandagainststalking.com website provides helpful information for anyone who is being stalked.
- **Paladin** is a charity offering trauma-informed service, to ensure that high risk victims of stalking in England and Wales are supported and that a coordinated community response is developed locally to keep victims and their children safe. Telephone: 020 3866 4107. Email: info@paladinservice.co.uk

Divorce & Child Residency (and see Legal Orders above)

- **Coram Children's Legal Centre's Child Law Advice Service** provides free legal advice and information on child and family issues www.childlawadvice.org.uk. Their Legal Practice Unit has limited capacity to take cases which require ongoing legal advice and representation and will usually only be able to take cases where legal aid is available www.childrenslegalcentre.com/get-legal-advice/child-and-family.
- **Law Society of England and Wales.** Provides a list of solicitors who specialise in family law near your location. (You must phone and ask if they specialise in domestic abuse). http://solicitors.lawsociety.org.uk/

Caring for Children after Leaving

- **Family Lives** national family support charity Website: www.familylives.org.uk/advice Confidential helpline 0808 800 2222.
- **Home Start** charity - national support for families with young children in difficult circumstances Website: www.home-start.org.uk
- **Family Rights Group** Support and advice if you are a parent, family member or friend of a child who has social workers involved in your child's life, or if you need extra support from Children's Services. Website: www.frg.org.uk/ Free confidential helpline 0808 801 0366 (Mon to Fri 9.30am- 3pm)
- **Single Parents UK** - an information site for anyone who is raising children on their own www.SingleParents.org.uk

....

Healing and Recovery after Leaving a Male Abuser

Helpful books

- **Refuge from Abuse: Healing and Hope for Abused Christian Women.** Nancy Nason-Clark & Catherine Clark Kroeger (2004) IVP Books.
- **The Emotionally Destructive Marriage: How to Find Your Voice and Reclaim Your Hope.** Leslie Vernick (2013) Publisher: WaterBrook Press.
- **The Verbally Abusive Relationship: How to Recognize it and How to Respond, expanded 2nd ed.** Patricia Evans (1996) Adams Media Corporation.
- **Boundaries: When to say Yes and when to say No - To Take Control of your Life.** Henry Cloud & John Townsend (2017) Zondervan Publishing.
- **Boundaries in Dating: How Healthy Choices Grow Healthy Relationships: Making Dating Work.** Henry Cloud & John Townsend (2000). Zondervan Publishing.
- **Called to Peace: A Survivor's Guide to Finding Peace and Healing After Domestic Abuse** Joy Forrest (2018) Blue Ink Press.
- **Divorcing a Narcissist: Rebuilding After the Storm** Tina Swithin (2015)
- **Eyes Wide Open: Help! with Control Freak Co-Parents** Dr. Debra A Wingfield (2014) CreateSpace Independent Publishing. (Some information on courts is for the USA but much of the rest applies everywhere).

Where to get support and information

- **Samaritans** 24-hour support for anyone experiencing distress, despair or suicidal thoughts. Freephone 116 123 (UK & Eire) Email: jo@samaritans.org Website www.samaritans.org
- **Victim Support** a charity that provides support and information to people affected by crime, including domestic violence and sexual abuse, as a victim or a witness. The website provides details of local support branches. Freephone 0808 1689 111 (Mon to Fri: 8pm to 8am, Sat to Sun: 24 hour service). Email: supportline@victimsupport.org.uk Website: www.victimsupport.org.uk

Counselling Services

- **NHS talking therapies** www.nhs.uk/conditions/stress-anxiety-depression/benefits-of-talking-therapy/
- **Domestic Violence UK (NHS)** domesticviolenceuk.org/nhs-post-can-i-get-free-therapy-or-counselling/
- **Women's Aid information on emotional support** www.womensaid.org.uk/the-survivors-handbook/emotional-support-and-counselling/
- **British Association for Counselling and Psychotherapy (BACP)** www.bacp.co.uk for information about different kinds of counselling or to find a private practitioner
- **British Association for Behavioural and Cognitive Therapies** www.babcp.com click on "public" for more information about CBT or to find a private practitioner
- **EMDR Institute** www.emdr.com for more information about EMDR or to find a private practitioner

For peer or group support for domestic abuse

- **Restored Online Network for Christian Survivors** of domestic abuse. Contact info@restoredrelationships.org for more information or to join this community
- **The Freedom Programme** website: www.freedomprogramme.co.uk a course which teaches about domestic abuse in a group with other survivors or online if there isn't a local one for you

Support for children

- **The Hideout:** website created by Women's Aid giving support to children and young people affected by domestic abuse www.thehideout.org.uk
- **ChildLine** Confidential telephone counselling service for children about any issue. Helpline: 0800 1111 (24 hour) Website: www.childline.org.uk
- **NSPCC** For anyone who needs advice, help or information regarding a child's welfare and for those who want to report concerns they have about a child or young person at risk of abuse. Helpline: 0808 800 5000 (24 hour) Email: help@nspcc.org.uk Website: www.nspcc.org.uk

- **Young Minds** Information for both parents and young people on mental health, including podcasts on the website and useful publications, leaflets.
Website: youngminds.org.uk Parents information service: freephone 0808 802 5544

Support for problematic drug and alcohol use
- **Alcoholics Anonymous** Helpline: 0800 9177 650 Email: help@aamail.org
Website: www.alcoholics-anonymous.org.uk for more information or to find a meeting
- **Al-Anon UK** Al-Anon Family Groups provide support to anyone whose life is, or has been, affected by someone else's drinking.
Free helpline: 0800 0086 811 Website: www.al-anonuk.org.uk
- **Narcotics Anonymous** Helpline: 0300 999 1212 (10am to midnight)
Website: www.ukna.org including local group finder

Support after Sexual Exploitation in Relationships/Marriage
- **Rape Crisis England and Wales** freephone **0808 802 9999** www.rapecrisis.org.uk
- **Rape Crisis Scotland 08088 01 03 02** (Every day, 6pm to midnight)
- **Domestic & Sexual Violence Helpline Northern Ireland 0808 802 1414** open to all women and men affected by rape or sexual violence, including friends and family of victims and survivors. Email: 24hrsupport@dvhelpline.org
- **Partners of Sex Addicts** Resource Centre www.posarc.com
- **The Naked Truth Project: WholeHearted programme** for spouses of pornography users thenakedtruthproject.com/wholehearted/landing

Support for lesbian,gay, bisexual and transgender people
- **Broken Rainbow** www.broken-rainbow.co.uk 0300 999 5428

Support for women and children from minority communities
- **Refugee Council** www.refugeecouncil.org.uk 020 7346 6777
- **Immigration Advice Service** www.iasuk.org 020 7357 6917
- **Muslim Community Helpline** www.muslimcommunityhelpline.org.uk
020 8904 8193 / 020 8908 6715
- **Jewish Women's Aid Helpline** www.jwa.org.uk 0808 801 0500
- **Kiran:Asian Women's Aid** www.kiranss.org.uk 020 8558 1986
- **Chinese Information and Advice Centre** www.ciac.co.uk 020 7692 3697
- **Latin American Women's Aid** www.lawadv.org.uk 020 7275 0321

Local Service Providers
- **Northamptonshire - Eve** (Transforming Lives affected by Domestic Violence)
www.eveda.org.uk 01604 230311
- **Birmingham - Pathway Project**
www.pathway-project.co.uk 01543 676800
- **Liverpool - The Crossing Point**
www.thecrossingpoint.co.uk 0151 378 9517

Specialist services

English as a Second or Other Language

- Ascent-Advice and Counselling offers free, confidential advice and support by phone, email and in person in a confidential space in every London borough. Individual counselling and support groups are also available across London. Services are available in a number of languages, including: English, Turkish, Punjabi, Urdu, Hindi, Bengali, Spanish, Portuguese, French, Farsi, Arabic, Kurdish, Dari, Pashto, Cantonese & Mandarin. This project also provides free and confidential legal advice, information and training and assistance for women with No Recourse to Public Funds. Access via Solace Women's Aid www.solacewomensaid.org or freephone 0808 802 5565

Support for people with learning difficulties

- **Respond** works with children and adults with learning disabilities who have experienced abuse or trauma, their families and supporters. Email: admin@respond.org.uk Website: www.respond.org.uk

Support for people with disabilities

- **Living Without Abuse** www.lwa.org.uk 0808 80 200 28

International sources of support

- **Hot Peach Pages** - International Directory of Domestic Violence Agencies www.hotpeachpages.net
- **Chayn** has country-specific platforms to help women easily navigate their options and exercise self-help escaping abusive relationships, plus tool-kits: open & free guides made with domestic abuse survivors around the world, particularly UK and Pakistan https://chayn.co/
- **RAINN** operates the US National Sexual Assault Hotline, accessible 24/7 by phone (800.656.HOPE) and online www.online.rainn.org.
- **The Laurel Centre** for understanding sexual addiction and support for partners in the UK, Holland & Dubai www.thelaurelcentre.co.uk/about-us

Theological Issues Relating to Domestic Abuse

Helpful books

- **God Hates Abuse: Abuse and the Doctrine of Headship and Submission.** Robin Mullins Senger (2016) CreateSpace Independent Publishing.
- **The (Un)Common Good: How the Gospel Brings Hope to a World Divided.** Jim Wallis (2014) Brazos Press.
- **Breaking the Silence on Spiritual Abuse.** Lisa Oakley & Katherine Kinmond (2013) Palgrave McMillan.

- **Healing Agony: Re-Imagining Forgiveness.** Stephen Cherry (2012) Continuum International Publishing Group.
- **Forgiveness and Reconciliation in the Aftermath of Abuse.** Christopher Cocksworth (2017) Church House Publishing.

Notes